"ALL THIS FOR A LITTLE GOLD"

The Diary of Henry Hawley, a Young Miner

1860 & 1861

Compiled by Betsy Buck

2015 Compiled by Betsy Buck

The diary of Henry James Hawley is reproduced here not in its entirety. Some entries are omitted, and headings are added to provide easier reading. The spelling, grammar, capitalization and punctuation remain as he wrote it.

❀

The original diary is the property of the
Colorado Historical Society, Denver, Colorado

A copy is available in the Colorado Western History Collections
at the University of Colorado, Boulder, Colorado.

❀

Illustrations by Betsy Buck

Printed with the assistance of:
Business Connection
Nederland, Colorado

Contact Betsy Buck at b.buck@mindspring.com

ISBN: 978-1-329-540668-8

DEDICATED TO

MARY HAWLEY SASSE

An important part of my Hawley diary adventure was meeting Mary, Henry's great-grandniece. From our first meeting began a comfortable friendship. We had in common our endless enthusiasm to unearth pieces of the life he lived.

It has proven to be fascinating, fun and with a lot of surprises. Exploring his hometown, Argyle, Wisconsin, brought us in touch with Henry's early years. Mary could produce articles, photographs, and history of the family. When she visited Colorado, we roamed Central City together, acquainting ourselves with the life he had led there. When exploring the gulches where he had lived and mined, we could imagine the joys and frustrations he must have felt as he pursued his dream.

A high point for us was discovering his original diary after assuming it no longer existed. We could hold it in our hands and read it, aware of the hardships it had been through as it kept Henry company every day for those years.

Thank you, Mary, for sharing your Henry Hawley with me!

Betsy Buck

ORIGINAL HAWLEY DIARY

Colorado Historical Society
Denver, Colorado

Mar 1st Thursday. A splendid day. The New M. E. Church is finished and dedicated to day by Mr. Mather from Mineral Point. had a very large congregation from most all parts of the country. I had a buggy ride P.M. accompanied by Miss Wyman. Mr. Sims preached in the evening commencing a protracted meeting.

Mar 2d Friday. Gloomy morning not much stir about tavern. I busied myself fixing up the garden fence choping wood and waiting on the girls. Manse a young gentleman who has been stoping here for a short time left for Janesville. Meeting in the evening. I am sorry to say that Mother is very sick.

Mar 3d Saturday. I went to Monroe with the Mail to day Mrs. McDermit with me. heard some large stories took dinner at the American House. Arrived home in good time. Had a very interesting meeting at night.—

Mar 4th Sunday. He card three sermons to day the Presiding Elder Mc Lawson preached are not very good success in getting mourners yet.
Mother is no better which is sad news.

Mar 5th Monday. A fine morning for business Father leased his mill to a man by the name of Howard. Charlie and Albert drawing hay. Uncle Anothny Millenbue from Wyote. came very near seeing a fight between Mc Dermit and transman but the thing would not go off. Meeting in the evening as usual.

Mar 6th Tuesday. ... warm to day Father went to Monroe no settlement in town. Uncle Lewis & Aunt Marie Sergent were down to see Mother who is better to day Had quite an exciting time at meeting this evening several went forward. Mr. Waldron gave us a good and interesting sermon and I judge it took good effect.

FIRST PAGE OF HAWLEY'S DIARY

Colorado Historical Society
Denver, Colorado

CONTENTS

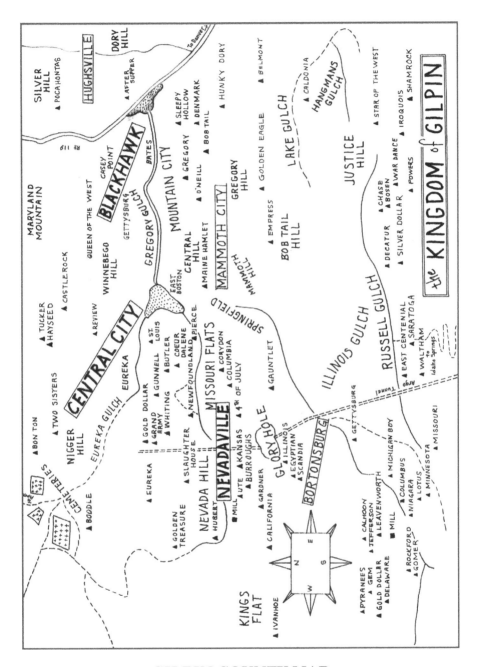

GILPIN COUNTY MAP

From "Guide to Colorado Ghost Towns and Mining Camps"
by Perry Eberhart, Swallow Press, Athens, Ohio

FINDING HENRY HAWLEY

By Betsy Buck

A tattered little magazine caught my eye at a used book sale. Published in 1953, it contained articles and stories about Colorado history. As I thumbed through it, I was drawn to a collection of excerpts from a diary written by a young pioneer in the 1860s. I started reading it, and became fascinated.

The author of the diary, Henry Hawley, barely out of his teens, wrote with candid innocence, intelligent insight, and playful humor. Each day, for almost two years, he faithfully reported on the life around him. From the first entries, I could detect his restlessness and boredom with living in his small farm town in Wisconsin. He longed for something else... was it a passion for adventure and excitement? Or was it the dream of striking it rich in the gold fields of the Rocky Mountains?

At that time, excitement was in the air about going West, mining for gold, and striking it rich. However, miners were returning home and telling their sad stories of hard work in the mines for meager rewards. Here, Editor William Byers of the Rocky Mountain News, in 1859, warned:

> *"Weigh well before determining to risk your chance... in search of virgin gold. Look around upon the pleasant home, the invaluable home comforts, and the many loved friends you are leaving behind; and then glance your eye forward to toiling days and freezing nights, pelting storms and the nomadic life you must brave and endure for months or years to come. Your bed will be upon the damp ground, your kitchen and dining room beside a fire of smoking, smoldering logs, and your place of daily labor in a gulch... knee deep in water and mud, icy cold, or else down in a dark cheerless pit.*

"You may be successful, or you may not. A few hundreds or many thousands of dollars may be your reward; or you may wander and labor for weary months for the bare subsistence with an uncertain and delusive future."

But young Henry didn't heed that advice. He eagerly made his decision to leave home and travel West with his uncle in the spring of 1860.

And me? I located a transcript of his diary and started a journey of my own. As I was pulled into the diary, my imagination took me back in history to the mid-1800s. I could picture the covered wagon lumbering along the prairie road, pulled by the team of horses, carrying young Henry and his uncle. They were confident and ready for anything! "Anything" meaning the hot sun, fierce thunder and rain, and even snow storms in May! Looking for their vagrant horses. Blowing sand stinging their faces. How could Henry be so cheerful all the time?

But his diary said, "I think that leaving home and crossing the plains is not as much fun as I thought it would be."

Upon finishing the diary, I was eager to piece together Henry's life. I had questions. When I found answers, I had more questions. What was life like as he grew up? What were his relatives like? Were there pictures? How did his life play out? Did he return home discouraged as most others did? Or did he stay? And why?

My main research centered in Colorado, around Central City. Following his day to day entries in the diary, I wandered the gulches where he had lived. Now, 150 years later, I found them bare except for some remnants of old mines, mills and cabins. Along with the huge rusted equipment there, they all told their stories. One discovery led to another. I visited museums, and couldn't keep away from libraries where books and computer gave me sparse, but important information.

Henry was hiding, but when I kept hunting, I was in for

some interesting surprises. I was taken to "Justice Hill" where Henry had witnessed a hanging. Another time, when wandering on the outskirts of Central City, I came upon a Hawley reunion! There, I became a celebrity, being warmly welcomed and acknowledged by his descendents for my ongoing interest in Henry. The diary described the twenty-foot waterfall he accidently rolled down, and following his description of its location, I found it. I could almost hear "the boys" laughing at him, and Henry thinking it wasn't so funny!

My curiosity has pulled me into numerous enticing situations. Most have been educational, many have been fun, and some a little scary, but I have loved every minute of these adventures, usually with the diary in hand.

I ask myself, "Why?" Why did an innocent discovery of an old diary pull me away from my normal life and put me into such an engrossing and irresistible search?

I know it was and still is a passion for me. And when one asks "why" to a passion, there is no answer. You just follow.

Now, for your own enjoyment, I give you Henry Hawley's diary.

Diary

March 1, 1860
to
December 31, 1860

Getting Restless

March 1st Thursday. A splendid day. The new M. E. church is finished and dedicated today by Mr. Mather from Mineral Point. Had a very large congregation from most all parts of the country. I had a buggy ride in P.M. accompanied by Miss Wyman. Mr. Sims preached in the evening commencing a protracted meeting.

March 2nd Friday. Gloomy morning not much stir about town. I busied myself fixing up the garden fence, chopping wood and waiting on the girls. Franse, a young gentleman who has been stopping here for a short time, left for Janesville in P.M. Meeting in the evening. I am sorry to say that Mother is very sick.

March 3rd Saturday. I went to Monroe with the mail today. Mr. McDermit with me, heard some large stories, took dinner at the American House, arrived home in good time. Had a very interesting meeting tonight.

March 4th Sunday. Heard three sermons today, the presiding Elder Mr. Lawson preached on, not very good success in getting mourners yet. Mother is no better which is sad news.

March 5th Monday. A fine morning for business. Father leased his mill to a man by the name of Howard. Charlie and Albert drawing hay. Uncle Anthony Miller here from Wyota. Came very near seeing a fight between McDermit and Vanarman, but the thing would not go off. Meeting in the evening as usual.

March 6th Tuesday. Quite warm today. Father went to Monroe. No excitement in town. Uncle Lewis and Aunt Marie Sargent were down to see Mother who is better today. Had quite an exciting time at meeting this evening, several went forward. Mr. Waldan gave us a good and interesting sermon and I judge it took good effect.

March 7th Wednesday. A beautiful day. Charlie went to Monroe. I did not much of anything. No excitement in town. Business dull. Meeting in the evening, preaching by Mr. Waldran. Mother a little better.

March 8th Thursday. I feel extra well today for some unknown reason. As usual, nothing happened worth recording today. Miss Mary Brown was down to meeting, she stayed with Louisa. A number went forward tonight.

March 9th Friday. Wind blows very hard, but not cold. I went up to Wyota with Andrew Anderson, not knowing whether I would return soon or not. Stopped at Uncle Louis' and then went over to town from there to where Henry Sargent was mining and down to Mr. Schellinger's, stayed there some time and then concluded to go back home and take a new start some other day, went back with Andrew. Meeting in the evening.

March 10th Saturday. Wind subsided this morning, air warm and pleasant. Albert went to Monroe this morning. I was quite busy most of the day pasting books for Dr. Thurston. No excitement in town. Meeting afternoon and evening, which I attended.

Henry's Decision

March 11th Sunday. Did nothing but attend church this fine day which was three times. A few went forward in the evening which gave new courage to the preachers.

March 12th Monday. I wrote three letters and did not do much of anything the remainder of the day only think what I should do the coming summer which did not amount to a very large sum. Meeting in the evening.

March 13th Tuesday. Meetings by the wholesale about thirty went forward this evening no excitement or nothing doing in town but meetings.

March 18th Sunday. Rained quite hard most of the day and all night. Meetings as usual 26 joined the class today. Not but a few out in the evening on account of rain. I went directly home as a good boy should.

March 19th Monday. I am getting tired of this staying at home without making anything. So I took the Walker's line and went to Uncle Lewis Sargents and the subject of "Pikes Peak" soon came up which I soon got interested in and some what excited in thinking of land which milk and honey flow but had not much idea of going.

March 20th Tuesday. Wind blows very hard this morning and I felt rather more like staying in the house than running around after my yesterday's walk. So I contented myself by carefully winning three or six of Mothers goose-eggs, which were fine. Fire built which soon gave them a warm reception after which we took of them a very hardy meal. Consequently I was not very hungry about noon which seemed to trouble Mother. But I never said goose egg and I hope when she traces these lines she will know the reason of my not being hungry.

March 22nd Thursday. Pikes Peak still in my mind and I do not see much of any show for speculation here. So I started for Uncle Lewis'es to see what arrangements I could make which I was not long in doing and we soon had our minds made up to see the Rocky Mountains and went to breaking a cold in the way of getting ready for a start soon.

Succeeded finely. I stayed all night, played chequers with my cousin until bed time.

March 24th Saturday. Stayed at Uncle Anthonys in the fournoon. P.M. Morgan and myself went down town to a town meeting and from there we went to Mr. Pitt Stafford where we had a very good time as Pitt is always full of jokes.

March 27th Tuesday. Sol favored us with his countenance all day which makes it very pleasant. I hung some meat up to smoke for Rocky Mountains which begin to make me feel kind of serious which I say nothing about.

March 28th Wednesday. Went down to Monroe with Nelson Gibson had a very windy day. I got some things for the trip. No excitement in Monroe. Meeting in the evening which is rather an old story with this journal.

March 29th Thursday. Got my boots half-soled A.M. and went up to Wyota P.M. Mother with me. Uncle and myself made some arrangements for the Mountains quite anxious to get started for I think that will be a tug of war with Mother. But I am soon away.

Preparing For the Trip

March 30th Friday. This morning finds us all well at Uncle Lewis's. Wind blows very hard still, and quite cold. I helped fix up a pair of harness and a number of other little jobs that were necessary to be done before leaving for the wilderness. Mother and I came home in the evening. Went to Meeting at church.

March 31st Saturday. Very pleasant this morning. Uncle Lewis came down this morning to get his team shod. We got a wagon cover which took me and the girls all day to make it and then I got a painter to paint it after night so as to have it ready for use. Girls very busy making shirts for the Rocky Mountains. I stayed at home as there was nothing going on in town exciting.

April 1st Sunday. A splendid day. I put the razar to my face this morning for the last time until I see the mountains. Went to church this morning for the last time for some time in the city of Argyle. Read most of the time during the afternoon and retired quite early as I have quite a days work before me.

April 2nd Monday. Quite cold today. I went from Mr. Mullins to Mr. Browns where I stayed some time. Had a good sociable time and returned home and spent the rest of the day in fixing up to make my exit from Wisconsin which I find is four times the work that I expected although I have plenty of help from Mother and Louisa who plead hard for me not to go so far from home. Which took very good effect although I keep it concealed as I had my mind made up to go and go I must which I may regret in some future day. Retired late a little tired.

April 3rd Tuesday. The last day of my stay at home has made its appearance which is a lovely one. I went up to Osborns Mill after my school money which I got without any trouble. I came back by Mr. Barrys and bid the family farewell. From there to Mr. Browns again where I had a time biding them good by but I soon found myself on the way home which I reached at noon. I bid a good many of the young ladies adieu during the afternoon which made me feel rather blue as I now begin to realize my situation in leaving a good home, society and all that I hold most dear, to go to the wilderness where I must for a time be deprived

of all such enjoyments. But I braved the storm quite well.
I shall not say what time I retired for I do not know.

Westward Ho!

April 4th Wednesday. Raining quite hard this morning. It
is hardly necessary for me to note the scene of leaving a
home that I have had so many enjoyments at. But suffice
it to say that my freight was soon in the wagon I bid them
all farewell goodby and started. Many were the thoughts
that popped through my mind during the night about the
past and future. I retired being six miles from home this
first day.

April 5th Thursday. The horses were soon before the wagon which they did not fancy very much, but we concluded
a thousand miles travel would bring them in good terms
with it. Traveled over high prairies until noon where we
took our first out door meal which consisted of boiled ham
and bread that went delicious as my appetite was rather
good about now. Camped the night. Uncle Lewis full of
jokes, therefore we had a good time and retired quite early
sleeping in the wagon. 32 miles.

April 6th Friday. Frosty this morning and cold. This getting out of bed out doors in a cold morning without a fire
is anything but fun for me, but I managed to live through it
and soon found us traveling a westward course over rough
country passing the morning. We crossed Mississippi River
on a ferry boat and stayed in Dubuque two hours, done
some trading. Camped early a little tired. 30 miles.

April 7th Saturday. Passed by several towns during the day.
I mailed a letter in one. We camped at a farm house where

we enjoyed a splendid supper gotten up by myself and consisted of ham and eggs. 35 miles.

April 8th Sunday. Passed some beautiful farms and a number of covered wagons all bound for the Mountains. Passed by Cedar Rapids. I should judge there were four or five thousand inhabitants in the city. Traveled on and stopped in good time. 25 miles.

April 9th Monday. Raining quite hard this morning and during the night. One of the horses got loose at midnight which caused me to get a little wet in finding it. Traveled over hilly country, roads very heavy which causes the horses to lag. Camped at a farm house. Plenty of company but all have ox teams therefore cannot travel with us. Heard some fine music in the evening. Saw a lady. Heard a story and retired. 28 miles.

April 10th Tuesday. Passed twenty wagons, traveled away from any wagon we got in contact with. Camped at a farmhouse where they had five hundred sheep. 32 miles.

April 12th Wednesday. We can see teams this A.M. as far as the eye can reach before and aft... all bound for the new Eldorado. No danger of being lonesome today for there is something new to be seen all the time which is the beauty of traveling. We reached the capital of Iowa, Fort Des Moine where we stopped to see the city. Got my hair shingled close to my head so as to be ready for the plains. We broke our wagon today but fixed it so as to last until we reach the next town. Knotts and Uncle Lewis all good at the stories. 27 miles.

Leaving Home Far Behind

April 13th Friday. Did not start early this morning for we now begin to notice that our team cannot stand everything therefore we intend taking it more moderate. I notice that we are leaving home far behind. We camped early only travling 25 miles today.

April 14th Saturday. Traveled twelve miles without finding water or seeing a house which appeared like going through the wilderness. Camped on a very high hill where wood and water was scarce but got along fine by using a few fence rails. 30 miles.

April 15th Sunday. Wind blowing very hard this A.M. and we traveled over high prairie all the fournoon. I walked ahead of the teams most of the time. Camped at a farmhouse where we heard some nice music, vocal and instrumental which caused me to think of home. Well rested. 18 miles.

April 16th Monday. Wind blows so hard this morning we have to take our wagon cover off. We traveled in company with twenty or thirty teams because we could not get away from them. Our road was very hilly and no timber. Passed several stage stations. We camped together and some ladies were rather inquisitive about my mode of cooking which I explained to them satisfactory. And maybe learned them something. 28 miles.

April 18th Wednesday. We had a very hilly road to travel over but did not last long as we reached Council Bluffs at 10 O'Clock A.M. At the Bluffs crossed the Missouri River on a steam ferryboat. The river is a mile wide and very muddy. We soon came to Omaha situated a mile west of the river quite a city and the capitol of Nebraska Territory.

We have traveled 16 miles today and by reviewing my journal I find that we have traveled thirteen days and layed by one. Cross is going west with us. I enjoyed my trip through Iowa very much and am well satisfied with what I have seen. Hundred of teams camped here.

April 20th Friday. We bought our outfit today which consisted of provisions of most all kind, horsefeed and a little clothing. There is a great amount of business done here as this is the last chance for getting goods and there are thirty to fifty teams leaving here every day.

April 22nd Sunday. Took a walk up the river where I saw a little of everything to excite my curiosity P.M. I went up to the capitol building accompanied by Alderson, Kelso and the Ladies. In the evening we went up to see a lot of Indians that were camped above town got them to wrestling and laughed at them until I almost cried. Got back and read a little, talked and retired thinking over my days work which has not been the best.

April 24th Tuesday. This is our last day at Omaha therefore all hands busy preparing to start. We loaded up our wagon, tried our new team which went splendid and got them shod. I bought Ellen's three girls each a present and made Ellen a present of a gold dollar to buy what she wished.

April 25th Wednesday. A fine morning. I am most dead with the toothache. Went to a dentist and had it filled. Everybody in a hurry and we were soon ready to start at noon. We bid Ellen good by and were once more on the road which seemed quite natural travling over high and rolling prairie all the afternoon. We reached hom river at sundown where we camped. They had a dance at a hotel close by but as I felt quite unwell did not indulge but retired early a little dissatisfied with "Pikes Peak." 23 miles.

Traveling a Hard Road

April 26th Thursday. Got an early start passed any amount of teams from all parts of the states. We had two wagons and everything convenient. Walked when we choose to as our load was light. We rode most of the time, came in sight of the Platt River which we are to follow until we reach the mountains. It is a large stream and runs very rapid. Had a good camping place at night and a jovial time around the camp fire. 32 miles

April 27th Friday. Crossed over on an iland where we took dinner, saw a number of Indians, one wanted whisky. I gave him a peper sauce bottle which did not suit him, shook a foot at me, gave a huge yelp and started off a short distance and called me to him and showed me a paper telling me that he was chief, good man me. Whisky. We left the iland and traveled until night over a fine road which was completely crowded with teams camped by a small stream called Cleon Creek. 30 miles.

April 28th Saturday. Mr. Cross waked us up this A.M. before day and informed us that the horses had taken a stampede and gone back down the river. We could do nothing until daylight when three of us started after them. Wind blowed very hard the sand with it. After traveling back to the ferry (15 miles) we met the four horses coming back, a man riding each one, which was a pleasant sight for our team is the main stay. We were not long in getting back to the wagons after eating a hearty breakfast for we had not had any. We started but the wind blew so hard that we could not go far. Camped early. 15 miles.

April 29th Sunday. We started quite early for a better camping place. Most of the teams are laying up. Camped at 3 O'clock had quite a lonesome time as most of the boys seemed to be thinking of Mama. 26 miles.

April 30th Monday. We were up in good time and every body ancious to be travling toward the Mountains. I have not seen a house for the last fifty miles which seems like a wilderness. As yet we have seen no game as it is most too early in the season. Uncle Lewis takes care of the horses and I do the cooking which suits us both. 28 Miles.

May 1st Tuesday. 28 Miles.

May 2nd Wednesday. After a little inquiry I learned that we were not far from Fort Kearny which we soon reached it being the first fort that I ever saw. It was quite a novelty to me. The Government had a number of soldiers stationed there also a fine lot of horses. After which we wended our way slowly westward. 25 Miles.

May 3rd Thursday. 28 Miles.

May 4th Friday. We had a little fun with one of the boys who we call Muslin (on account of his telling about his muslin shirts every day) as he is afraid of thunder and as it thundered very hard this A.M. We could not get him out of the tent so we took it from over him, he ran from there in the wagon where he stayed until the thunder was over. Our road today is close by the Platt river we are now travling on the plains where Indians are without number also houses for there is none, except now and then a stage station. Everything appears to be a little wild. There are thousands of teams on their way to Pikes Peak therefore we have company all around us, but everybody for himself. 30 Miles.

May 5th Saturday. We had a jovial old time with Muslin today as he is the laughing piece for us. We had a splendid camping place, plenty of wood, water, grass and company. After going a visiting, I retired. 27 Miles.

May 6th Sunday. 21 Miles.

Braving the Storms

May 7th Monday. We got an early start this morning and continued until 2 O'clock when the wind commenced blowing very hard and cold which caused everybody to make use of their overcoats. Camped early on account of wind which we could not avoid as there was not a house or tree insight. It commenced hailing, raining and snowing before bedtime. All right but the poor horses. 28 Miles.

May 8th Tuesday. A day long to be remembered for the wind is still blowing carrying the snow with it which is drifted around our wagon so that we can not leave it, the tent and four men entirely covered up, the horses are only twenty yard from the wagon but we can not see them on account of the snows blowing so hard. I was the first one out, uncovered the tent so the boys could get out. I then went to the horses which had tramped the snow down until they had it three feet deep. I could not help them any only to pity.

So I made tracks for the wagon which I reached almost frozen. I was soon into bed again where I was glad to stay until noon when the storm broke away.

We all made our exit out of bed and cared of the poor horses the best we could also got some breakfast which we were very much in need of as we did not get much supper. Some of the boys thought going to Pikes Peak was a hard road to travel, Muslin came very near giving up. I thought that leaving home and crossing plains was not as much fun as I imagined. But we all made the best of it we could. Saw any amount of men hunting their teams. P.M. had as much fun as could be expected.

May 9th Wednesday. The wind is still blowing quite hard and the snow is very deep in places where the wind cannot get to it. We started this A.M. early passed teams and wagons all day without any cattle or horses as they had all ran away. Saw one mule that frose during the storm. Our teams look rather hard. 30 miles.

May 10th Thursday. Got an early start as Uncle Lewis counts one hour in the morning worth two at night. Still passing wagons without teams, a few men are left to guard the wagons while other are hunting the teams. They look rather down hearted for a team is a man's main dependence in this wilderness country. Stoped early giving the teams a fine chance to recruit up a little which they need. Read some *Shakespeare* in the evening and retired. 22 Miles.

A Hunting Misadventure

May 11th Friday. Started this morning before sun up saw for the first time a few antelope. We stoped at noon and Seth Hamilton and myself took the guns and started a hunting off to the bluffs three or four miles from the river. We soon came to the game. I got three or four good chances to shoot but the old gun wouldn't do it. Therefore we gave up the chase without success and started for the wagons where I learned that my gun was not loaded to my great dissatisfaction. We were soon on the road again and I was glad to ride the rest of the day. 30 Miles.

May 12th Saturday. Today we have travled in sand knee deep all going a foot. The wind blows very hard carrying the sand with it which makes it very dissagreable travling. Saw a four horse team run away without doing any harm such stampedes occur often on the plains. We Are passing teams all the time. Camped early. 30 miles.

May 13th Sunday. I am my own man today, although a long ways from Dady, being twenty one years old. We can see the Mountains for the first time which looks like a white cloud. We are 860 miles from home and almost to the end of our journey.
30 Miles.

May 14th Monday. These are high sand hills and covered with fine timber and good grass. It is the first timber that we have seen for 180 miles. Indians here by the hundreds all chiefs are beging but they don't get much. 33 Miles.

May 15th Tuesday. We had a very steep hill to climb also sandy roads all day. Freight wagons are numerous coming and going. Indians thick around the wagons but were soon scattered. 30 Miles.

May 16th Wednesday. When we stoped to let our teams feed I thought I was not quite satisfied on the hunting line but coaxed Hamilton to go with me and we started for the bluffs full five miles from the teams. I had a fourteen pound gun (loaded this time) soon scared up a drove of antilope which we chased around over the hills until we were almost tired out not thinking once that the wagons had started on as soon as we started a hunting. We gave up the hunting without success and started for the road as it was almost noon and we were very thirsty. We soon reached the road, could see nothing of the wagons but heard they were two hours ahead. Therefore we had nothing to do but make tracks which we did as fast as possible. Reached Ft. St. Vrain 2 O'clock where we tried to get refreshment, as we were very hungry, but they informed us that they had nothing to eat. We went on and reached the teams at sundown. Tireder boys never lived for we had carried heavy guns all day without anything to eat and not much to drink. Uncle Lewis thought we were ahead and drove faster than usual to overtake us..therefore we could not blame them. Soon we retired perfectly satisfied with hunting on the plains. 25 Miles.

May 17th Thursday. Much as ever that I can get up. I did not go a hunting today. Cross and I stayed in the wagon hardly looking out all day therefore did not see anything. Camped within ten miles of Denver City. Had a fine day and roads. All ancious to see the City which is most to our journey end. 25 Miles

Journey's End

May 18th Friday. Some of the boys dressed up in their best this A. M. Muslin especially. Started quite early and passed some splendid ranches which I like the looks of very much. Arrived at Denver City at 10 Oclock A.M. Much larger place than I expected to see, it is situated on the east side of the Platt River and is fifteen miles from the base of the Mountains being a Market place for the gold mines in the Mountains. Auroria which is west of Denver Cherry Creek dividing the two places which is dry most of the time is also quite a business place. I saw for the first time an Indian dance which was rather a savage sight as they were all painted ready for battle which they soon expected to have with another tribe. We left Denver 5 Oclock P.M. and went out to Clear creek toward the Mountains where we camped for the night. All the boys with us except Hamilton who hired out at Denver as a blacksmith. Horses look well. 15 Miles

May 19th Saturday. A beautiful A.M. We concluded to lay up today and prepare for a Mountain journey by way of setting wagon tires, washing, mending, and cooking. Tried to shoot prairie dogs without success. Did not run around very much.

May 20th Sunday. A splendid day. I took a walk up the creek a short distance saw a few fine ranches which are called farms in the states. Got back and read the rest of the fournoon. All being ancious to reach the Mountains we started a little afternoon passed by Arapahoe quite a village where we see for the first some gold mines. Arrived at the foot of the Mountains at 4 O'clock. My first object was to see the top which I started for three or four with me, who soon took the back track except one. We traveled on not thinking it very far, but we found to our sorrow that it was almost dark when we reached the top... therefore took one glance around. Saw Denver the Plains and a huge mass of hills. We were told there was a fine lake on the Mountain but had not time to go to it. After hard climbing down we reached the wagons content with mountain climbing. Camped in the Mountains a long way from home. 10 Miles

May 21st Monday. Started early having a different road to travel over today being in the Mountains soon reached Golden City. Did not stop but went on and soon came to Golden Gate (every thing has the name of gold but I have not see any yet) where we had to pay toll on the road. After leaving the gate we travled up a canon seven miles when we found ourselves at the top of a high Mountain where we took dinner after which we went down the Mountain that was so steep that I expected to see the whole apparatus go end over end. There were rocks in the road as big as a hoss, (a great road to pay toll on), which we lifted the wagons over. Camped early and tired only travlling 15 miles. Anything but a Mountain road.

May 22nd Tuesday. Up bright and early cold enough to freeze eggs which is not very pleasant. Got a start and traveled up a hill perpendicular four miles, a big story, but almost true. Came to what is called the Four Mile House and then went down a hill similar to the one we came up... only not quite so much so, and before I knew it we were at the celebrated gold mines Gregory's Gulch which is quite a sight. Found a number washing dirt in the gulch that looked very rich. We camped half way up the gulch and sent our teams back to the valley on a ranch. So are ready now to make our fortunes or be found trying. There are a few Quarts [sic] Mills running which crush the quarts that are raised from Lodes on the Mountain side. Only one Steam Mill here the rest water Mills situated on Clear Creek (North). Some of the boys left to find work. Retired quite late thinking of a far distant home. The end of our journey. 10 Miles

Launching the Mountain Life

May 23rd Wednesday. All up bright and early this A.M. and with our pick, pan, and shovel started for a little prospecting tour. Went over a high Mountain, passed what is called Missouri Flats, Illinois Gulch and around by Nevada Gulch. We found hundreds of men working in the gulches all making the ready dust and wanting to sell out. After seeing all we wished to for one day returned to camp. P.M. Uncle Lewis and myself went around to see some of the Mills which he thinks can be improved with a slight expense as he is an engineer. We camped in Mountain City which is composed of a few very respectable log buildings and a few not so respectable. But a few ladies here but heap of bachelors some of them rather rough customers as every mining country can boast of. Sunday and churches are not known here in the Mountains. Therefore if I am rather rough in my style it will or must be excused.

May 25th Friday. This fine A.M. found us up early and soon were on the trail for South clear Creek eight miles from Gregory. After passing up spring Gulch, over Missouri Flats across Illinois Gulch we came to the head of Virginia Gulch which we followed down near three miles and arrived at Clear Creek. Took our lunch on the bank of the living stream after which we proceeded up the creek where there was considerable mining going on. We met Knott & Co. who we had not seen since leaving Omaha. After having a hearty shake of hands and look around we started for the wagon where we had a fine supper and exchanged a few stories. We retired sleeping in an old cabin without any door or chinking.

May 27th Sunday. We find it a little frosty this A.M. as we did not bring our coats with us. In the P.M. we went up Eureakee Gulch, dug two or three prospect holes without getting a color which is rather discouraging. Retired early a little tired of prospecting.

May 28th Monday. Wind blew very hard most of the night and is snowing very hard this A.M. and continued to all day which prevented us from leaving the camp very far. Teams are coming in every day and the mountainsides and gulches are completely covered with tents and wagons. Some of the pilgrims feel rather blue.

May 29th Tuesday. Cleared off fine. We all started out again, travled over a Mountain three miles high which took the breath away from us a little as the air is much lighter than what it is at the Missouri River on account of being several thousand feet higher. We climbed a mountain almost perpendicular where we saw very good signs of a lode (Blossom rock) and we went to work sinking a hole and worked faithful for eight hours without finding anything but hard rock. Got back to the wagon, almost gave up. Prospecting for gold is anything but fun.

Where's the Gold?

June 4th Monday. There was a Gent came to us this A.M. and wanted to sell us a claim over in Lump Gulch eight miles from Gregory which would prospect 25 cts per pan. So Uncle Lewis and myself started quite early travled up the long Mountain which we came to get here until we arrived at the four Mile House. We passed two beautiful lakes and soon reached the celebrated gulch which we were disappointed in for we could hardly raise the color. Therefore we told Mr. man we were not buying claims today which make him feel rather blue as he thought he had us about sold. Walking sixteen miles over these Mountains is anything but fun.

June 5th Tuesday. Went to Hinkley's Express office this A.M. and got a letter from sister Louisa which was quite acceptable as I had not heard from home since leaving it. Theater at Hadly's Hall in the evening which is a log building close by camp.

June 6th Wednesday. We talked a little of buying a claim in Russels Gulch and walked over one or two high Mountains did not see anything but huge rocks. There are four to five Steam Mills coming in every day and are being set up in most all the gulches.

June 7th Thursday. This fine A.M. we concluded to take our packs, which consisted of grub for two days, blankets, pick, shovel and pan and start for a gulch that had never known a pick. We went out by the Four Mile House and most to the lakes where we found the gulch. We went to work sinking a hole, Cross and I digging and Uncle Lewis panning. Worked hard most of the day without finding a color and came to the conclusion that other men were sensible in passing by without digging. We started back and soon reached Missouri Gulch five miles from Gregory where we found a fine waterfall of twenty feet that I undertook to slide down and found myself rolling down in double quick time which was not very pleasant for me but fun for the rest.

June 8th Friday. We bought a claim on Russels Gulch this A.M. which we are to pay $100 for. Giving a wagon down and the balance after all expenses are paid. Other miners were at the camp and they talk of going home to see their "Sallys." Lots of them talk of going back to America.

A Roof Over Our Heads

June 9th Saturday. Uncle Lewis, Rogers, and I went down to our claim in Russell's Gulch this A.M. and prepared to build a cabin in the way of digging a foundation and cutting logs. Prospected the claim a little and got a good color. P.M. returned back to Gregory which is five miles from the cabin.

June 10th Sunday. I went over to Shockly's camp. Saw Hoyland who is bound for home. Most of the men run their sluces [sic] all the week and clean up on Sunday therefore most of the business is done Sunday.

June 11th Monday. We started this A.M. gag and baggage for our new home which suits me for I am getting tired of climbing these Mountains without finding anything. On account of the team not being very true we were seven hours going five miles went backwards most of the way. We concluded not to build a cabin but fix up our tent which we did. Uncle Lewis sleeps in the wagon and the others in the tent. All retired early at our new place.

June 12th Tuesday. Up early this A.M. warm and pleasant. The men went to making sluces and Uncle Lewis and I went to digging a drain ditch which has to be done before working our claim on account of water. We paid twelve cents a foot for lumber to make the sluces with. I found it everything but fun standing in cold water ankle deep all day with the hot sun pouring down on us.

June 13th Wednesday. All went to work. I find it not very agreeable. Give me the old home instead of being in water ankle deep in the Rocky Mountains. Many men started home today.

June 14th Thursday. Feel rather old this A.M. I do not know how Uncle Lewis feels as he pitches in without any complaint. Uncle Lewis went up to Mountain City and settled some trouble without difficulty.

June 15th Friday. The sluces were finished today which are 100 feet long all of them having long riffles in except the one to throw dirt in. We will now have more help in the water. Any amount of men working above us, teams coming and going all the time from and to the states. It would not take a very large amount to start me but such thoughts must be banished. I am glad to see the end of the week come if the times are blue. Quit work early.

Waiting for Letters

June 17th Sunday. A beautiful A.M. and day. I went up to the P.O. where I found all the men in the Mountains waiting for letters each one taking his regular turn. Mine came in the course of time without receiving a letter. I returned home.

June 19th Tuesday. I jumped a claim this A.M. Uncle Lewis went to hunt Knotts'es team. Found them on a ranch. All worked as usual. Lots of men are commencing work below us therefore we have company enough.

June 20th Wednesday. Finished the ditch today which is two hundred feet long and from one to ten feet deep. Cost us $60. P.M. we set our sluces and run through considerable dirt, got a good prospect which is more encouraging than digging ditches.

June 21st Thursday. I went up to Mountain City this A.M. after a sluce fork which I paid $5.50 and letters which I did not get. I got back at noon washed dirt all day and did not get a speck of dust. Cold night.

June 22nd Friday. I shoveled dirt in the sluce all day which is anything but easy work. Knotts staked me off a quarts lode claim in Virginia district. Hands are very scarce, wages $2.50 a day. No coin to be had, nothing but the ready dust and not much of that.

June 23rd Saturday. Nothing happened A.M. worth of not. All worked as usual. P.M. two men got into a quarrel about jumping a claim, drawed revolvers but did not pull trigures, therefore no one was hurt.

June 24th Sunday. On account of no where to go and not wanting to do anything we did not get up very early. I read a very little during the day in *Pilgrims Progress* and the *Bible.* P.M. I went down the gulch until I came to North Clear Creek. Walked about five miles.

June 27th Wednesday. A beautiful A.M. everything passed off fine with our sluce boxes until noon when the men below us made a dam across our ditch causing the water to back up on us so that we could not work. We all went down to tear the damn down or be found trying but we had no trouble and were all soon back at work. P.M. it rained and hailed very hard. I understand by the old Mountaineers that the rainy season has just commenced, which will last some time.

Rain, Rain, and More Rain

June 28th Thursday. Rained very hard for an hour or more this A.M. but didn't hinder us from doing a very good days work without receiving very much profit. It hailed very hard just at sun down covering the ground three inches deep.

June 29th Friday. Cloudy and sprinkled a little. I did some washing as we have to do our own washing as there is not a woman in hearing which I do not admire very much. Had the rheumatism for the first caused by working in the water so much. Rained.

July 2nd Monday. Rained during the afternoon enough water to run the sluices today. P.M. the wall that I stood next to which is ten feet high caved in and caused me to jump over the sluice boxes and into a hole of water waist deep just in time to save myself for the sluice boxes were entirely covered up. Prof. Knotts allowed that I was quite active which done him to gas about for a long time. Also fun for others. Rained tonight.

July 3rd Tuesday. Rained very hard. Took us until noon to dig our sluices out, got them placed and ran through a pile of dirt. On account of being in the water so much I feel quite unwell, but not so that I cant work. There are some ladies camped near us that helps to drive dull care away. Rained.

July 4th Wednesday. Very warm. The rest of us went to work cleaning out the ditches which the rain of yesterday filled up. We got everything all right by noon and worked a short time when it commenced raining and continued to all the afternoon, filling up the ditches, pits, carrying off sluices which is very discouraging. Rained tonight.

July 5th Thursday. Quite warm. We got everything straited up by noon and as we did yesterday, just got to slucing when one of the finest and hardest rains that it has been my lot to witness this summer made its appearance washing everything away which it came in contact. We are wet all the time. Some of the boys look rather blue, therefore

I kept on the bright side, but it was like tearing out an eye. Gold mining is anything but fun.

Discouraged Miners

July 6th Friday. Very warm and water scarce so that we can not do much today. Cross got back from Mountain City without any letters. Immigration is about done for this year except freight wagons and returning pilgrims. I should like to hear from home.

July 7th Saturday. Got to work this A.M. before sun up. We found no regular pay streak as they do above us and in other gulches, but the gold is very fine and scattered. To-day we have been washing and scraping the bed rock which is from two to eight feet from the surface and as a general thing the largest quantity of gold is found on the bed rock and in its crevices. Three of us washed out an ounce and twenty cents today. Rained.

July 8th Sunday. I went up to Mountain City P.O. did not get any letters, as usual. Very few pay regard for the Sabath as most of the gulches are being worked also mills running, teams coming in. We had mince pie and fruit cake for dinner. Returned early and read. Rained.

July 9th Monday. Knotts and Cross accompanied by several others, started over the range this A.M. The rest of us went to work slucing as usual. P.M. cold, cloudy and rained. A dreary old country if they find nothing. I shall be almost tempted to start for America.

July 12th Thursday. A disagreeable A.M. Raining quite hard but soon cleared away and we worked until noon when it commenced raining very hard and continued so to do all the afternoon. The water came down the gulch six or eight feet deep filling up ditches, pits, and making the sluce boxes travel which perhaps caused a few hard words just to ease the mind for ready dust can't be taken out tonight. Such is a miners luck.

July 14th Saturday. I dare not look toward the claims this A.M. for I presume they present a horrible aspect for it rained quite hard most of the night and during this day. I commenced to read the *Bible* through but do not know how far I will get.

July 16th Monday. This morning we took courage to see how much the rain storm had favored us. Found that it would take us three days to place every thing in running order again. I worked in water knee deep all day. I have a severe head ache all day and if I was at home nary work. I concluded that I would not work in the water any more. Uncle Lewis agrees with me therefore we are Majority.

July 27th Friday. As we bachelors have our own washing to do, I concluded to do a little this A.M. Newton is making a pair of pants. Most of the Men are leaving the Gulch. We talked of selling. Rained.

July 28th Saturday. We concluded to turn the water off from the claims and put them in a better shape for selling, which we did. I took a walk upon a high mountain where I saw a grand sight below me vis a very hard rain storm while the sun was shining bright and warm where I was. Also had a fine view of the plains and the snowy range. Read a little I should like to get a paper and hear some state news.

July 31st Tuesday. We are in hopes to sell out before many days. We concluded to take another tramp. Uncle Lewis and I went up to the City, took Dinner, and went to the office and got three letters which I paid 75 cents for. All well at home. I promised myself not to return home until I can take more money than I brought away which will not be much. Farewell to July. May the next one find me in better health.

Thoughts of Leaving

August 1st Wednesday. Our neighbors below sold out this morning for a fine sum to a man who knows a little more than the common run. I guess he will not know quite so much after working his claim a while. We are in hopes to sell out before many days. I am on the sick list today. Uncle Lewis sluced a short time and got six dollars and thirty cents. Rained hard.

August 2nd Thursday. I feel rather unwell this A.M. The rest sluced a part of the day. There were two different men here to buy which is encouraging. Uncle Lewis went up to see what they had to purchase with. I feel a little better. Rained during the day.

August 3rd Friday. We have the good fortune to sell out for what we called four hundred dollars in wagons, oxen, rifles, revolver and sugar, also a little coin. All is well that ends well. I am out of the gulch which suits me but we have to wait a short time for the part of our pay. If I had a little more I would leave the Mountains.

August 4th Saturday. I made out the papers this A.M. but we do not have possession until Monday. Rained and hailed.

August 5th Sunday. Everything all right this beautiful A.M. Uncle Lewis went up to Lake Gulch. I read and walked most of the day. I am in hopes of having the pleasure of leaving this dull place before many days. Rained.

August 7th Tuesday. Not much to do therefore I took a late paper and climbed the highest mountain I could find and enjoyed its contents without being molested. Our successors are troubled a little with water. I find this more agreeable than being in the water every day. If I only understood Geology I might make this journal more interesting as this is a grand country for that science. Weather beautiful.

August 8th Wednesday. Although far from home and deprived from the society here in the wild of the rocky Mountains, I enjoy myself to a considerable extent. The Mountain sceneries are interesting and there is something new to be seen most every day. The people here are from all parts of the States and most of them have different habits, especially the Southerners. I hear nothing about politics out here as every body is for money and not for office, but unless the mines yield better I think there will be a few office seekers before long.

August 9th Thursday. Nothing much to do, So I started up to mountain City a pedling a few bottles of diamond cement which I soon disposed of at cost as it was out of my line of business. I should like to see Cross & Knotts come back. I think if they find nothing I will bid the Mountains farewell. Took dinner at a bakery. Got back and it rained and hailed.

August 10th Friday. I concluded to hire out a day or two and commenced this A. M. at $2.50 per day. Our successors are still working but get discouraged a dossen times a day. Nothing exciting happened. Rained a little.

August 12th Sunday. Is a day which is not respected any more than any other by a large class of the miners as they sluce all the week and clean up on Sunday... i.e. take the gold dust out and pan and retort it ready for circulation. A great many gone after raspberries. I had a fine mess for supper. Read a little. Rained as usual.

Tug of War

August 13th Monday. Did not do anything but read and cook today. Uncle Lewis went up to Mountain City to see if he could hear of the boys but did not. A.M. it was very warm but P.M. an overcoat was quite comfortable as it was very cold. Rained.

August 14th Tuesday. Uncle Lewis and I went up to the P.O. I came home and on my way met Knotts just returned from his prospecting tour. His reports of the southern mines are rather discouraging. Cross and the horses were over to Calafernia, Georgia, and several other gulches which are over the snowy range and about 160 miles S.W. Now if our claim buyers could settle with us I would begin to think what I shall do next. Rained very hard P.M.

August 15th Wednesday. The water came into the lake this A. M. from the ditch and it not being properly fixed the water broke over, coming down the gulch at a 2-40 rate about four feet high and twenty wide washing every thing before it which caused a few hard words to be uttered. The weather is cold and disagreeable.

August 16th Thursday. We all went to work in the claim this A. M. helping to open it again from the great wash which it received yesterday and to get our pay. Very warm a part of the day and rained and hailed P.M. The nights are cold. Gold dust is not to be had out of some of the claims. Uncle Lewis and Knotts think of leaving for America soon. I hardly know whether to go or not. Retired early.

August 17th Friday. All went to slucing this A.M. but did not work long before our successors paid us in a wagon which they got from another man and we discounted $40 on this paper. A number of Wyota boys took dinner with us. They were on their load for America. P.M. we settled up and Cross went down to Burgess Ranch after oxen. Rained.

August 18th Saturday. Today we are preparing for America. We soon got our baggage in the wagons and bid farewell to our old stamping ground and went up to the Lake where we camped for the night. Knotts went over to Clear Creek & I saw John and George Schellenger. Got back quite late and slept in the wagon as I have done all summer.

August 19th Sunday. Now comes the tug of war whether I must go home or stay in the Mountains. Uncle Lewis offers to take me free of charge which is a better offer than I will get again. But I have not got quite enough dust. I bought the oxen and wagon from the company, paid $75 and bid them good by. Uncle Lewis, Knotts & Cross and Newton are going to stop in Gregory district and I took my team and went up to Schellengers. Rained.

A New Beginning

August 20th Monday. I hired out a short time at $1.50 per day and board to John Schellenger. The latter and myself went to work in the Iowa Lode close by the cabin. There is no crevice in sight. John ran around and did not do anything. I find it much better working in dry ground than working in wet. I went out to see my cattle in the evening on a Mountain. Rained.

August 21st Tuesday. George and I went to work in the lode. We have not much of a crevice yet. P.M. I went to drawing quarts with one team, and John took my cattle and drawed lumber from a saw mill up on a high Mountain to timber up shafts with. I drawed quarts from the Rounds'es Mill in Russels Gulch. Quarts is on porrous rock which is found in lodes varying from three inches up to six feet in width also varying in richness. The gold is obtained by the aid of quarts Mills which run by steam and contain from six to twenty four stamps weighing from four to eight hundred each. This country is well supplied with Mills. In the evening I fixed my bed which consists of Rocky Mountain feathers (pine boughs). Rained.

August 22nd Wednesday. Worked on the lead today but not very hard. P.M. George wrote a letter to his Alice. In the evening John wrote a letter and I read, what time I was not troubling the boys. No rain.

August 23rd Thursday. This beautiful A. M. finds George & I about twenty feet under ground working hard for the ready dust when we find it. I was favored a short time with the tooth ache, but a lady being close by who was quite a doctress, I soon found relief. No rain.

August 24th Friday. I think the rainy season is about over. The days are fine and warm and nights are cool. The atmosphere light on account of being several thousand feet above the level of the sea. P.M. I hunted cattle. Went over to the P.O. Letters are something that I am not very intimate with at present.

August 25th Saturday. George and I prospected for a lead today without success, although we worked hard. John ran around to find some lodes to stake claims on. He found one, the Kansas Lode, and staked each of us a claim which may be a fortune to us some day.

August 27th Monday. I went over to see the Kansas lode which is on what is called a hog back on account of the peculiar shape of the Mountain. John went over to Nevada Gulch with Smith. Three of us worked a prospecting this day without finding any thing. I notice that mony is a hard substance to get hold of even in this gold country. Looked for my cattle.

August 30th Thursday. The boys talk of renting a part of a claim on the Topecia Lode. They want I should go in with them, but I had rather work for them a while longer and see how the thing navigates. I found my oxen. In the evening John and I went down to a dance only a short distance but did not indulge.

August 31st Friday. P.M. I did not do anything but prospect the lead that the boys have rented and play chequers with John. Rained and hailed very hard. Goodby Mr. August of 1860.

Gunshots

September 1st Saturday. Clear and warm. There was quite a miners meeting in the gulch today in regard to holding claims. John went down to the office but did not get me any letters. We had a lady dine with us today which was quite flattering here in the wilderness.

September 3rd Monday. I notice that a person is willing or rather obliged to do most anything here to make the ready dust. John drawed wood and I drawed quarts and George worked in the Benton Lode which they have lately rented. Weather fine.

September 4th Tuesday. The boys commenced work on the Topecia Lode this A.M. and gave up the Benton for the present. I drove team and drawed quarts. Another mill started up in the gulch today. The Indians are rather hostile to the Denver people I hear but do not place much confidence in it. Business lively but mony scarce.

September 6th Thursday. I have been trying to study up some plan to make mony a little faster, but as yet have not succeeded, for this working by the day is slow pay. Drawed quarts A.M. and chopped wood P.M. The gent was here to buy my oxen and wagon but could not raise the dust.

September 7th Friday. Cloudy most of the day and rained quite hard at times. John worked on the lode. George partly made a wood rack and I chopped wood which is a high calling. How long this will last I am not able to say but I think not long. Gloomy day.

September 10th Monday. Rained steady all night and continued most all day. I was around over the Mountains looking at lodes. We started down the gulch to meet Newton as agreed upon a week ago and settle a little difficulty but as they had all deserted except Drake. We soon were on our road back by lake Gulch and then home after a walk of ten miles. John and George received three letters from home. I not any as usual.

September 12th Wednesday. I went to work on the Lode with George and Smith had fun as well as work. Raind. There are ten mills running in the gulch and not any of them making more than expenses, which makes times rather hard. Night cold enough to make it not agreeable sleeping.

September 14th Friday. I concluded to board myself and by so doing make fifty cents more on the day. The credit system is being carried on here extensively and unless the lodes prove better than they have minus would supersede plus in the day of settling up. Weather quite cold. Mittens and overcoat are comfortable. Played chequers with Smith.

September 16 Sunday. A romantic scene occurred near the cabin this A. M. Vis a woman drawed a revolver on a man and would of shot him if the thing had of gone off but it was no go. She tried the second time. John and I went and found the oxen. I wrote a long letter home. Our neighbors below fired over a hundred shots from revolvers during the evening. So much for a Sunday.

September 17th Monday. We all went to work on the lode this A. M. except John who made a door to the cabin. A committee formed a resolution to hang a Lady and gentl-man tonight but up to bed time no body was hung.

September 18th Tuesday. Pistols firing and men a shouting all night, no one hurt or hung this A.M. Cloudy and cold and disagreeable all day. I drawed quarts. Nothing exciting going on today. Very cold at night.

Missing Home

September 21st Friday. Up bright and early this A.M. Cold and cloudy still. Went after my team and drawed quarts all day and cleared $6.60 which is a little more en-couraging. Wind blew very hard carrying dust with it.

September 22nd Saturday. I was sick all night but am all right this A.M. Drawed quarts from the Calhoun Lode to Davis'es Mill. John went down to the bob-Tail Lode in Gregory district to see about taking some specimens home, as he expects to start soon. John had the ague when he got back.

September 23rd Sunday. Wind still blowing. Several in cabin during the day. I went down to the office without success, got a letter for John. George wrote a letter to his wife. I think it's a grand thing not to have a "sally" to trouble a person while he is in the wilderness. John agrees with me and George thinks we are perfectly out of our heads. Better times past and I hope better coming.

September 27th Thursday. Cloudy most of the day. Snowed hard on the range today and raind here. I drawed quarts from the Benton Lode cleared $7.00. John bought nine gallons of Molasses at $2.00 per gallon. Bought a newspaper to send home which was printed at Denver City. Evening beautiful, warm and pleasant.

September 30th Sunday. A beautiful day only a little too warm. George and I went up on a high Mountain which is directly in front of our cabin where we had a fine view of the plains and Snowy Range, Clear Creek and the Village of Idaho. Got back very tired and not at all contented.

October 1st Monday. A beautiful A. M. for the first of the month and being in the Rocky Mountains where the weather can change in five minutes from better to worse. John is travling over the Mountains to find something that there can be something made at.

October 2nd Tuesday. John and I started to make our fortuns today... or rather to discover a new Lode. We are on the side of the Mountain above Missouri City and dug all day without finding anything and then returned home concluding to try another day. We fixed up the cabin. I wrote a letter home and retired. Cloudy. Hailed, raind, snowed, and thundered.

October 4th Thursday. Wind blows extra hard and continued to all day. P.M. I did not do much of anything but run around and see what is going on which is not much of any thing but work. Read a little during the evening. I am just about give out tonight.

October 7th Sunday. A splendid day. If I could be at home this A. M. I think I could enjoy myself more than it is possible to do out here for churches, good society, and morals are strangers to this country. Every body came out here to make mony therefore Sunday is the business day. Stores are open, Mills are clashing away pounding out the dust and the gulches are lind with men running the dirt through the sluces and this is the way we get our mony. I went over to the office as usual I got no letters. I read most of the day.

Preparing for the Long Winter

October 11th Thursday. Today we helped John to fix up the wagon for Denver as we intend to buy our winter provisions there. John went after the ox again and gave him up for lost. Made some stools, fixed the table and prepared to live as bachelors ought to. I drawed poles to finish my hay yard, banked up the cabin and hunted for the lost ox without success.

October 13th Saturday. We worked on the Wastman until noon and then went over in Nevada Gulch district and staked off some claims on the Ready Pay lode. I staked one for Charles as well as myself, came back by the office and George got two letters from the U.S. Mail as it has lately been established in the Mountains. Returned home quite tired after a hard days work.

October 17th Wednesday. We worked all day on the lode, the prospect not very good. John returned from Denver in the evening with our winters grub consisting of a little of every thing in the way of substantials. Smith came with John bringing a can of peaches which didn't go bad. Dr Hart gave us a call and was rather tight I judge from the way he fell over the wood pile. Weather beautiful.

October 18th Thursday. George and I painted up the cabin inside and stacked our grub away. We are prepared for winter now, have everything that boys could wish except a cook stove which George says he will have before many weeks pass which is a good a thing as John and I want. I sent a bill for our provisions home.

October 21st Sunday. I was busy most of the day reading *Political Matters*, also a little in the *Bible* for a change. Nothing exciting going on. Our cabin is too comfortable to leave.

October 22nd Monday. We chopped seventy house logs. Smith was here doing some big figuring and had us all rich a talking but not working. He is good on the wind work. To be in fashion John made me a window curtain in the evening.

October 25th Thursday. We bought a fine cook stove which adds greatly to the warmth of our cabin, built the barn for the cattle and fixed up things in general for a long and tegious winter.

October 26th Friday. Got up this A.M. and found four inches of snow on the ground and still snowing. Which gives us a beautiful sight as we look at the snow covered mountains which are towering above us on every side. Stayed in the house most of the day and as we are bachelors did some sewing and washing. Snow six inches deep. I made a testator to tell the depth of snow that will fall during the winter. John tried to get up a dance but could not for the want of women. I wrote a long letter home which makes ten written home and only two received. Such is the life of a miner.

Things are Looking Up

November 5th Monday. This A.M. Smith is figuring big about renting a cabin on the Bent co Lode situated on quarts hill above Nevada. But cannot go into it without having help in the way of ready dust therefore we agreed to go in with him thinking nothing could be lost and stand a chance of making something. George was a little opposed to it. Signed for the *Rocky Mountain News.*

November 6th Tuesday. Weather is fine as I ever saw. Every man to his post...did not make much headway on the Bent as they have to build a cabin, find the crevice and all that before taking out any pay. I went to a law suit in the evening and was called on for a witness. A law suit in the Mountains is rather diverting as every man is his own lawyer.

November 8th Thursday. The wind whirling around every corner this A. M. it is impossible to tell what depth the snow has fallen. We piled out some fine looking quarts today which I think will pay very well. I sent Father two papers printed in the Territory.

November 9th Friday. I find it quite a task to keep a daily journal but must try and finish this year and perhaps next. I think us boys have got a good thing here in the Mountains in the way of claims for they certainly can not all fail. A half dossen visitors in the eve.

November 11th Sunday. I went down to the Express office in hopes of receiving a letter which was useless. I took a notion to go to church. No preacher came, therefore no meeting. Spent the evening pleasantly reading the N. paper.

November 14th Wednesday. Snow five inches deep on the level. We have four hands hired one on the Topecia and three for the Bent Co. There is some excitement about the New Mexico mines and a great many are leaving for that part which is about 400 miles south. We got the Presidential election returns from the Missouri river...in fifty-six hours a distance of six hundred miles Abe Lincoln of Illinois is supposed to be the President of the United States. No doubt but what they have had exciting times as Douglass and Breakenridge were also running for the chair. We know or care but very little about the politics in this country, therefore I do not keep posted as I should or ought to. Retired late.

Blasting

November 15th Thursday. Got up and went after the oxen before breakfast. Hired a hand to drive them at $20 a month. Several Mill Men were after our quarts to smash, did not promise any. Wrote letters in the evening.

November 16th Friday. Snowed hard and steady all day which is rather disagreeable as we all worked as usual. We had to blast for the first time today. John not very well.

November 17th Saturday. A beautiful day. The weather changes very sudden in the Mountains. The boys both sick today. I worked as usual. The oxen drawed house logs to build a house over on the Kent Co. which Smith is attending to. Read the *Rocky Mountain News* in the evening.

November 18th Sunday. Our cabin seems to be a regular rendezvous for a number of gents as there are always about a dozen in, especially on Sunday. Then I did not add much to my mental faculties in the way of politics today.

November 19th Monday. Snowed all day as usual. George well again. Nothing worthy of not happened. All quiet.

November 20th Tuesday. Quiet and cold. We engaged two different mills to do our crushing so as to give them a fair test. Nothing to do with the team so we set the driver to chopping wood. Cut my toe most off.

November 21st Wednesday. The boys went over to help raise the cabin on the Kent Co. We intend to board our hands. I went after the cattle at noon to draw quarts and commenced drawing. The weather resembles Wisconsin winters.

November 22nd Thursday. It snows regular every third day therefore it is snowing today. Grim drove my team to draw quarts and got about done. Read the ancient History in the evening. Wind blowing.

November 23rd Friday. This A.M. puts me in mind of the storm on the plains. As the wind is blowing a hurricane carrying snow, gravel and good size sticks with it and it is very cold. We did not think of going out doors as it is hardly safe. Several stoped in to warm. At dark there was hardly any snow to be seen as it had all blowed away.

Lady Visitor Adds Cheer

November 27th Tuesday. We got returns from our quarts today. Davis Mill got $45.60 and the Free Port Mill $109.40. Each had ten cords and the same kind after paying for crushing. We came out in debt but we are going to try it again if the Kent does as well we will keep trying.

November 28th Wednesday. Very cold. Got the oxen shod which costs eight dollars. Several left the gulch for New Mexico. I wrote Charles, Louisa, Albert & Theodore.

November 29th Thursday. A man here offered us $10 per day to draw quarts but found one of the oxen so lame from shoeing that he could not travel, therefore we are minus that much each day. I read the daily News which is printed at Denver. Weather warm and pleasant for a change.

November 30th Friday. We begin to learn that renting lodes is uncertain business. We talk of buying a claim on the Hill House but the price is rather too much. Some of the boys were in during the evening and we had a social game of euchur to pass the time away. In the Mountains here where we are deprived of good society as a general thing we become rather rough in our style, manner, conversation and it is not strange if we should be a little wrekless.

December 1st Saturday. Worked until noon and then went to Central City bought a pr of boots and mittens which I paid $8 for. Returned home by the Kent County which looks rather gloomy but I think if rightly managed will be all right.

December 2nd Sunday. Finer weather I never saw for winter. Not any snow on the ground and quite warm. Had a lady visitor today, Mrs. Rowlins that added a little to the cheerfulness of our bachelor circle. Evening John read *Ida May*, George read the news paper and I read the ancient *History*.

December 5th Wednesday. Wind blows hard but not cold. Three of us on the Topecia. John trying to discover another lode. Got Joe Grim to help him. I got another claim today. Times are quite dull at present in the Gulch.

December 7th Friday. I felt more like staying in bed than going to work but as George is sick I must go in and work my sickness off. Alex fighting mad because his blasts did not do any better.

December 8th Saturday. I did not sleep much on account of the tooth ache all night and continued to until noon when I went to a Dr. to have it extracted and in so doing he broke it off also loosing another so that I am in rather a precarious situation as far as eating and comfort is concerned. Went down to the office and got four letters one of them for myself directed in Johns name written by Mother and the first that I have received since last July.

December 9th Sunday. I feel rather large around the jaw this A.M. and I cannot chew any thing therefore have to let any thing alone. I went and found the oxen all right. I wrote a short piece in Borise album. I commenced a letter to Mother and read a little. I am leading a little different life than I expected to when leaving home in regard to meetings, and society.

December 10th Monday. I think last night was the coldest that we have had and it is quite cold today. I am working although not able. Others working.

December 11th Tuesday. Smith went over after a keg of powder which we got from C. H. Gratiot and paid $14. My tooth quite painful yet. John broke the wagon.

Farewell to 1860

December 14th Friday. Things are conducted very poorly and I am afraid that it will run us behind but it is impossible to get out at present as we have not money to pay the hands off. John drove a pick through his foot while working in the Topecia. I have the tooth ache again. Mr. Sinclare from Denver is stoping with us tonight. He thinks the Mountains are all right and when they get to saving gold better this will be a rich Mining county.

December 15th Saturday. I did not rest very well on account of the tooth ache. I drawed quarts, saw several wagons smashed down which is nothing strange. Sinclare here at night. He has been trying to purchase an interest in the Free Port Mill. I feel miserable at night.

December 16th Sunday. I did not get far from the cabin today. I heard there was Meeting in the gulch but I am hardly a fit subject to attend church. John not able to do anything. Snowing.

December 17th Monday. I acted the woman a while by ironing as the wind blows so that it is almost impossible to get out. Moderated a little P.M. And I Went over on the Kent Co and settled up with Smith. Found that our expenses up to date have been $470.90 with no income yet. That is the way the mony goes. I find this a hard way of living.

December 21st Friday. I went over on the Kent co and put a cabin over one of the shafts and left as quick as I could get away. Snowed and blowed most of the day. No letters.

December 22nd Saturday. I did nothing but run around this day. Got some grub and took it over on the lode A.M. I wanted to see how the boys were doing found them doing about as they pleased. To Central City to see a set of blacksmith tools and then to Mountain City P.O. and got home a little tired.

December 23rd Sunday. Cold last night but clear and warm today. Davis in the cabin thinks he knows more than most of people and will not read a northern paper for fear he will become an abolitionist as he is from the south.

December 24th Monday. I started this A.M. to open the boon Lode. Kendal furnished a hand and we are to sink a shaft between claims. John in the house as his foot is not any better. Rather dull for Christmas Eve.

December 25th Wednesday. Christmas did not agree with me from the way I feel this A.M. but I worked as usual. We got out some fine looking quarts. After I quit work I went down to Central City to have some recording done but was too late. I went home and after Tea went down to Pullmans Mill after the mony which I did not get and the gentleman and myself changed opinions and I bid him good night.

December 28th Friday. I heard the wind howling around the cabin this A.M. long before light and it did not stop during the day. The range looks as if it was blowing away. We all stayed in the cabin today. John gave me a sentence in the *Bible* to read correctly which I did.

December 31st Monday. This being the last day of another year I have been thinking about my success since leaving home which is anything but encouraging for I might of stayed at home and enjoyed the blessings of good Society... fine parents... sister and brothers, also of improving my mental faculties far more than I have yet done. But forgetting the endearments of home, I have enjoyed myself to a considerable extent. As I always had a desire to learn the ways of the world by experience rather than by study and I find a trip one thousand miles west is quite a start for a new beginner. During the trip I had the pleasure of seeing men from most all parts of the U.S. I find that the men from the Northern States act talk and their habits are some what alike, while men from the southern States are not alike in their habits or do not resemble the Northern in the least. I could soon tell a Georgian or a Missourian from each other, much easier than I could distinguish one tribe of Indians from another. At the end of my journey I found myself in the Rocky Mountains where I have since been seeking for riches with thousands of others. Mining is the foundation of this part of the Mountains and I will stay another year or more. The day has been warm and pleasant and all passed off as usual. Good by A.D./60

CENTRAL CITY 1859-1860
Earliest known photograph of the city

Diary

January 1, 1861
to
December 31, 1861

A Shooting Affair

January 1st Tuesday. A beautiful day. I enjoyed myself Tip top working hard as the mode of recreation in this country does not suit my style Vis drinking fighting whiskey. I heard of a few parties but as I am living rather a retired life did not indulge in any of them. Rowlin came up quite late after George's revolver as he says his life has been threatened.

January 2nd Wednesday. We all went to work. There are fifty men at work in sight of me. There is a car that is used for drawing quarts in runing up and down the mountains and it ran off from the track today very near killing a man. Went to Central City saw nothing exciting.

January 3rd Thursday. Worked until the middle of the afternoon when I was taken quite sick and started for home which I reached with some difficulty. Found John sick so we had a jolly time of it.

January 4th Friday. I am able to be around but not to work. Stayed in the house then went after the cattle to move Rowlans things away as one Davies talks of confisticating his wife, household goods & C. While I was watering the cattle Davis shot Rowlan through the head but not killing him. After some trouble the gent was arrested and is now the topic of the day.

January 5th Saturday. Great excitement prevails this A.M. in regard to the shooting affair of yesterday. Some are for hanging, others for whipping and some are for shaving his head, croppng his ears and numerous other ways were suggested in way of punishment but they are having a regular trial and will give him a fair show. Rowlan is not dangerously wounded. The boys were summoned to witness but not called upon. Boys got home at midnight. Jury were out trying to agree.

January 6th Sunday. Exciting times today. The jury gave their verdict as guilty and sentenced Davis to have one side of his head shaved, receive fifty lashes and make his exit from the Mountains for ever. The time soon came for the fun to commence. His head was duly shaved and then he was taken to the spot where he done the deed, tied to a tree and five men gave him his fifty lashes on the bare back that made him get up and stir about. There were eight hundred or a thousand men present all shouting to put it on harder but very few had any sympathy for him. The last that was seen of him was taking down the gulch at a 2-40 rate. The crowd then voted to have the lady of Rowlan banished also and gave her twenty four hours to leave in. This is rough business for a Sunday but such things have to be attended to. But such a day I do not wish to witness again as it adds anything but good to any one. All resumed its usual calmness in the evening.

Keeping on the Bright Side

January 7th Monday. This A.M. finds me all right for work. I went down on the Boon. John and George over on the Kent. Our prospects at present are not very flattering. There is rather a poor show for a fortune in the Boon as we have struck no regular crevice. Received a paper from home. Snowy and cold.

January 8th Tuesday. Snowed all night steady and all day. George went down on the Boon as there was blasting to be done which is out of my profession. I found my self over on the Kent among the wildest lot of boys that were ever permitted to collect together. Fourteen of them at work for us and they are not paying expenses. A stormy evening.

January 9th Wednesday. Every thing looks discouraging. Nothing goes as it should be but as Father says all for the best so I will keep the bright side toward me. I took some grub over to the hands. John still in the house which agrees with him exceedingly well. I am reading *The Life of Henry Clay* which is quite interesting.

January 10th Thursday. I am with the boys over on the Kent most of the time. We are raising one and a half cords per day which is clearing expenses. Pullmans Mill of Russels Gulch and smith and Chaffys Mill of Lake Gulch are crushing for us.

January 11th Friday. Weather warm and pleasant. I received a letter from Mother and Louisa that were quite exceptable as I have not heard from them before since Dec. 1st. Nothing exciting going on, no news from the States of interest. All well at home.

January 12th Saturday. Weather changes here about every ten hours. I had the pleasure of working fifty feet under ground this day. We are rolling out the quarts on the Kent Co. Read News Papers in the evening.

January 13th Sunday. Cold and cloudy and has the appearance of snow. Weather changes here about every ten hours. I went to church for the first time since April 1st A.D. 1860 and it had a very good impression on me for I thought of home and also that I am getting rather rough in my style, maners and perhaps a little wreckless. All of which can be easily accounted for when necessary. Amused my self with *the Bible* and *The Life of Henry Clay.*

Such is a Miner's Life

January 14th Monday. Went over on the Kent co early and found the grub about exhausted. Came back and went after the cattle and took 268 lbs beef to the boys which will last them a week. Our expenses are from 125 to 150 per week. I do not know what the income is. I was sick all over when I got home. George put a peck or less of ashes on my face for to cure the tooth ache. Snowed very hard all day. The boys mended their boots.

January 15th Tuesday. Very cold. The weather changes every ten hours. We all did our jobs. John stayed home to see about drawing some house logs.

January 16th Wednesday. Snowed steady all day. Every fellow in his place. I fixed a platform for quarts and went down to Nevada with the tools. Wrote in the evening.

January 17th Thursday. Clear but bitter cold today. We got returns from Pullmans mill. The quarts yielded $36 per cord which only pays for raising them saying nothing about drawing and crushing. Such is a miners life, therefore I will not complain but get out of it as soon as possible.

January 18th Friday. Cold and the wind is going at a high rate. Went over to the Kent Co with the intention of selling or giving out to Smith but could do neither therefore some other mode must be adopted soon. The hands could not work therefore they had a high old time dancing, singing and CC. Election in the District today to elect a judge...Rogers elected.

January 19th Saturday. I went down to the Boon with George today. Things look rather gloomy in that region.

The hands not at work today. I am almost gone up after the spree of yesterday.

January 20th Sunday. Wind blows very hard. John and myself went to meeting. We all went to prayer Meeting in the evening and I got up and told them that I should like to live a Christian life if possible, but as for receiving any change of heart I know nothing about therefore according to my Saviours doctrine I am not yet a Christian and I do not know that I ever will be but intend to live a moral life as near as possible treating every man as I should wish to be treated. By so doing I will have a clear conscience.

Thoughts of Home and Friends

January 21st Monday. I went over on the Kent Co to where everything appears dull. I think the thing will be closed before long. Perhaps any one reading this will think that we were poor business men for not closing sooner, but when I tell them that we have fifteen or sixteen hands who can not be turned off without either money or provisions when we can manage to board them and run the risk of our next quarts yielding more or until they can get suitable places to work else where. Mr. Boice is running for sheriff. We all went down and voted for him. Considerable excitement and a number of men decently tight. Took John and I until 9 o'clock to find the cattle again.

January 22nd Tuesday. Smith bought a claim on the Kent co for which he agrees to pay $1000 for. George and I went down on the Boon where if we had not done as much work I would be giving it up but perhaps we may strike something in a few days.

January 23rd Wednesday. This is one of those windy days that keeps a fellow in the house. I wrote some letters and read as long as I could see. I notice that they are having a warm time in the south about the presidential election and talk of some of the states secceeding. I think old Abe will put them on the square March 4th.

January 24th Thursday. George and I drawd up a fine lot of wood and done some washing. A number of the boys were over to see what was going to be done as they said they were little afraid that they would not get their pay but they left perfectly satisfied in that respect. Went to prayer meeting in the eve.

January 25th Friday. Very cold and windy. John and myself went over on the Kent Co with the intention of settling all up and giving the lease up. We soon found that we were $500 in debt to the hands. Could do nothing with Smith, therefore we left not at all satisfied. George and I had a great debate in the evening.

January 27th Sunday. Attended church twice and took a part. Had quite an argument in the evening with George about the literal heart being changed before a person can become a Christian. John and myself on the negative. We stopped the thing unsettled as none of us would give up. I retired thinking of home and friends and how long it would be before I could again be with them which was also not determined.

Cabin on Fire!

January 28th Monday. John and I took up our beds and walked over on the Kent Co to see if we could not straiten things up a little with the boys. Turned out two hands and took their places. I worked half of the day and night, the first night work I ever did. I had almost as soon be in prison.

January 29th Tuesday. I went after some provisions, saw George at Whipples. We were taking out the quarts quite fast by the cord instead of by the halves. No mail.

January 30th Wednesday. A hard place to get any sleep in as the cabin sets over the lode and they are blasting steady all night. Nothing exciting.

January 31st Thursday. Got up and went to see George. Found him on the John lode which we have rented. We do not intend to give up any thing but Smith. If one thing does not pay we will try another and so keep doing. Went and got tools sharpened. Good by Mr. Jan.

February 1st Friday. This month comes in quite cold and the snow fell during the day. We all worked as usual during the day and night. Had a little fun at noon with a Missourian who was very ancious to whip some one but came to the wise conclusion to cave in.

February 2nd Saturday. John and I throwed off our chains and left the Kent Co and returned to our comfortable cabin P.M. Election in the gulch for recorder as a few were not satisfied or in other words wanted the office but Fasset Jr. was the choice of the people. Went to meeting in the evening, heard a very good sermon. Retired well contented with our weeks work.

February 3rd Sunday. Nothing exciting to day... no meeting therefore quite dull as I never visit saloons only to see and not to indulge. Therefore I stayed at home. Went to meeting in the evening and when we returned found that our cabin had been on fire but fortunately some kind gent happened along just in time to save it or we would have been turned out of bed and home.

February 4th Monday. Windy and cold. We commenced work on the John Lode. We have one hired hand Alex who worked with me. John went over to straiten up things on the Kent. John got a parcel of letters including a dossin or two liknesses.

February 5th Tuesday. We fixed up the chimney A. M. that got burned down on Sunday evening. P. M. everything received its usual attention.

Scenes in a Bachelor's Cabin

February 6th Wednesday. John and I worked on the John Lode and George down on the Boon. All worked hard not knowing whether we are making our regular dust or not.

February 7th Thursday. Quite cold and the frost is flying in the air. P. M. snowed hard. We got settled up with Smith today. Found that we were in debt to him and hands $454. All is gone besides our own labor. In the future we will pull our own strings. John stakes some claims of the Gold Dirt Lode. George on the Boon struck a crevice that he thinks is a crop crevice but Kendal and John declare it is not, so time will tell.

February 8th Friday. Not but little snow on the ground. Kendel insures us that we have every thing all right in the money line, but I rather doubt his judgement. Times are very dull. Mill not doing much and money scarce.

February 9th Saturday. A beautiful A.M. We took out quite a lot of quarts on the boon. I wrote a letter home and directed it to Theodore.

February 10th Sunday. We went to church and found it not very interesting as there are but very few who take any interest in church matters. Found Mr. Sinclare and Mcdonald at home and also a number of other gents in through the day.

February 11th Monday. All pitched into work this A. M. as usual. George struck no indications to assure him of a main crevice on the Boon. George wanted to sell out but John and I wanted more or nothing and perhaps the latter will be our reward. In the evening Sinclare is with us and reading *Sewards speech.* George a shoe making. John a tailoring. I received a letter from Louisa and partly answered. Such are the scenes in a bachelors cabin on a winters eve in the Rocky Mountains. The weather very cold and wind coming from the top of mountains ends up in the gulches.

February 12th Tuesday. The New York co. are trying to persuade us to leave the Boon but I think as prospects are so flattering in our behalf that we will stick to the Boon at least a short time longer. Read during the evening. Seccession and disunion seems to be the feeling of the South.

February 14th Thursday. The weather too stormy to think of working, therefore we concluded to stay at home and wash. John chop the wood, I bring the water and George does the washing all works admirable. Went down in the gulch today where I saw several men under the influence of Bacchus and ready for a fight, therefore two of them went at it and fell through a window and conclcuded to wait until sober before settling up. Nothing exciting. Wrote Albert a letter.

Visitors

February 15th Friday. George and I went down on the Boon and I am satisfied that the crop crevice is one without a doubt. Bick drawd a cart of quarts to Pullmans Mill for us and John fed the mill and frose his toes. He is a lucky boy when there is work to be done.

February 16th Saturday. We had a number of friends to visit us on the Boon all of them thinking that we have our fortunes somewhere about. That is my opinion but so far about that it will take two fortunes to get it. Gloomy day.

February 17th Sunday. Cold and cloudy. John and I attended church twice to day. When we got home found McIntosh and Kennen there and Wear came home with us. McNight soon came in and not long after, a representative of Kansas came in who looks as though soap, water, and clean clothes had not been his fortune to contend with since leaving Kansas. As we were dining he said he would take a"tater" with us after which he made his exit to the great satisfaction of all of us. Read during the evening and wrote Louisa.

February 18th Monday. The air is quite still here this A.M. but there is a mighty roaring in the west which can be distinctly heard, and also reached us soon but was not very cold.

February 21st Thursday. There is no excitement going on except all are eager to receive the latest news from the States in regard to the South preparing to secede. We have had a variety of weather to day in the way of change... first warm and clear, second cloudy, third snowing, fourth wind and fifth stoped snowing and turned very cold toward evening. We have what reading matter that we have time to read.

February 25th Monday. Up bright and early and went over on quarts hill to get some powder for Kenner. From there to the Boon where I found the rest of the boys. All passed the day without complaining except Uncle Alex who was not able to work P. M.

February 27th Wednesday. We got returns from the Barnes mill this A.M. which were 3.20 per cord... encouraging sure... working for nothing and boarding ourselves. A rock fell from the top of the shaft and hit me on the shoulder which pains me very much to night.

February 28th Thursday. I have nothing of interest to mention to day. The Boon looks rather discouraging which is a common occurrence. Alex quit. Went to meeting in the evening. Good Day Mr. Feb.

Old Abe Lincoln

March 1st Friday. The first came in clear and calm but did not remain long before clouding up and snowed hard and steady all afternoon. Worked on the Boon with John. Retired early for want of lights.

March 2nd Saturday. We were all anticipating fine weather this month as it was so windy last month, but on getting up this A.M. I found the mountins decked with a white robe and fair prospect of more before night. Our hopes are blasted as far as weather is concerned. Concluded not to work so I commenced a letter to Charles. Read the ancient History in the evening.

March 3rd Sunday. Snow several inches deep. Old Sol gives us his countenence and is quite exceptable. George not well.

March 4th Monday. A blustery morning. Did not work today. I presume there is lively times in Washington as Old Abe Lincoln takes the chair in the White house. Signed for the *rocky Mountain News* commencing March 1st. George not very well.

March 6th Wednesday. George able to work and him and I went down to the Boon taking Kendal with us who we intend to keep with us until the thing opens out a little better. John stayed at home and did housework. Many mills are laying idle for want of water which the ditch fails to furnish during cold weather. Cloudy and has the appearance of snow.

March 7th Thursday. We are favored with a high wind and plenty of snow to day. I went on top of a high mountain after a drill. Came very near being blown away and started for the Boon and was glad to stop at Whipples where we made some ladders and then returned home where we found Wear and John enjoying themselves tip top.

March 8th Friday. The wind blows hard enough this A. M.to carry gravel stone without any trouble. I went down to the P.O. and then to Whipples where I stayed most of the day. Played fox and geese with the whole family except the old Lady, for the want of something better to do.

March 10th Sunday. There is a meeting but very little use when there is noise in the way of mills running, chopping wood, drawing quarts and wood, blasts a thundering in every direction and perhaps the next door saloon where drinking etc. is carried on extensively. Especially on Sunday where even a Methodist minister has no show of making noise enough to be heard. A.M. I went around Bald Mountain by following the ditch three or four miles. This mountain is situated at the head of Nevada Gulch and is composed of a huge pile of rock towering high above the surrounding mountains and contains no shrubry or trees which is the reason of its being called Bald Mountain. Misses Wm. and Laura Agnew were here P.M.

Mountain Beauty and Good Food

March 11th Monday. Weather changeable. I saw Frank Elder today who told me that he had cleared $1100.00 in twenty four days by working a claim on the Cotton Lode situated near the Bob Tail. The Boon received its daily labor. The Ladede Mill took $1400.00 from two cords of Pyrites of Iron. The mills are doing much better than six months ago. In the evening I went over into Virginia District to a miners meeting and was kind of fishing for the Recorders office but the old recorder was sustained.

March 13th Wednesday. The wind blows quite hard but not cold. We went down below taking P. C. Smith with us instead of Kendal. I went down to Mountain City to see about renting a cabin situated near where we are at work. I rented it for a short time. As two miles is most too far to walk twice a day as we have been doing for some time.

March 16th Saturday. It is so cold that the wind is not able to blow, the air is full of mist or snow and the trees have a coat of white and in taking a glance around me I see quite a romantic scene. Went down to Black Hawk Point after powder got a keg & let Whipple with me have half of it. Saw a water mill about crushing our quarts. Commenced snowing P.M. & continued so to do until I retired.

March 17th Sunday. Snow four inches deep. The wind blew very hard most of the day carrying the snow & gravel with it. Stayed in the cabin all day. J. J. Smith came over to celebrate his birthday bringing 2 cans of peaches and a bottle of Champain and of course we had a high time, suffice it to say Smith did not get away to day. There were several in the cabin during the day.

March 19th Tuesday. Could not think of going very far to day for, as I often have written before, the wind is blowing a perfect hurricane sweeping every thing before it. John went down to the office and got me a paper and almanac. Snowing quite hard in the evening. Contented in the cabin.

March 20th Wednesday. We had a team to commence drawing quarts from the Boon to a water mill this A.M. All worked as usual. To tell the truth we are getting rather short of grub more so than I ever was use to before but unless we see some rough times we will not appreciate a mountain life. But there is hope.

A Wandering Mind

Mar. 21st Thursday. We had everything as usual in regard to wind, work, and snow. They finished drawing quarts to day, one fellow triped over his wagon which caused a little profane language to be used. I stoped at a mill that Boiece has rented while returning home. Al Boiece was here in the evening. Wrote Louisa a letter and retired.

Mar. 23rd Saturday. A beautiful day. I went down to Gregory Point or Black Hawk Point to see if they had cleaned up. Found that the mill had frozen up. The rest worked as usual. I went up through Mountain, Central, and Missouri Cities all of them have improved very much within ten months passed. Nothing exciting in the evening.

Mar. 24th Sunday. George went down to Whipple's and accompanied P. C. Smith in a general tour around the mountains. John went to church and I took a stroll around a high mountain & soon came in sight of the plains. Also a beautiful chain of low mountains reaching as far as the eye can extend adding to it the beautiful stream of South Clear Creek and the snowy range and I had a splendid view. Here I sat down and as the day is warm and pleasant an hour was soon passed away in happy thought about home & friends far away. A number in the cabin during the eveing Sinclare among the rest who stayed the night with us.

Mar. 25th Monday. A sad accident happened near when I was at work on the Boon a log got started by some means down the mountain that is very steep, and hit a man killing him instantly..he did not see the log until to late. The Boon is still undeveloped and I am affaraid always will be. Stoped at the office and got two letters one from Wm Loveland and one from home all of Argyle.

Mar. 26th Tuesday. As we are out of Powder Fuse and money and not but very little grub we concluded not to work. So I went down & got our regular report from the mill which was anything but satisfactory for we expected to get $100 per cord when we only got $50 but we are used to being disapointed. I saw a very nice fight while returning home. I wrote Wm Loveland a letter & made some preparations to move down on the Boon in the morning. I retired thinking what I am a doing all for to get a little ready dust which will do but little good when under control and if I ever get out of the wilderness I will stay out.

65

Snug Little Cabin

Mar 27th Wednesday. George and I left John this A.M. for a time by taking up our bed and walking down to the Boon. Smith assisted us and we soon found ourselves all right in a snug little cabin on the side of a steep mountain & six hundred feet above the Gregory Gulch. Went down town and layed a supply of Powder, Fuse, and Grub. Worked P.M. all right. I do the windlassing & cooking and George & Smith do blasting. The day warm and pleasnt.

Mar 28th Thursday. After letting the boys down the shaft I went down town to see Dodge and get some dust which I accomplished easy. Saw J. J. Smith and J. Kennr in the coach going to Denver. Snowed hard P. M & blowed quite hard during the night. No excitement.

Mar 29th Friday. I went over on the Bob Tail Lode at a blacksmith shop got the tools sharpened and then went down to Mountain City after candles. We have plenty of company on every side of us and all jovial and full of jokes therefore time passes away swiftly. Windy & cold.

Mar 30th Saturday. The same routine followed to day as yesterday in the working line. Kendal was here at noon and appeared to be very much discouraged. George went up home in the eve to see how John is getting along.

Mar 31st Sunday. The last day of the month has rolled around bringing with it no change in our pecuniary circumstances. Smith went up to Whipples therefore I was left alone. I went no where saw nothing interesting but mountains and Gulches which occupied my thoughts most of the day in studying.

April 1st Monday. This beautiful A.M. finds me enjoying my self tip top. Sun shines very warm. The mountain side is covered with miners all going to their regular work. I am having an easy time as it is not much trouble for me to cook and I have but very little windlassing to do. Went off to Missouri City P.O. and got George a letter came back by Central City and got my paper which I read in the evening.

April 3rd Wednesday. A beautiful A.M. Every fellow at his post. I read most of the day. Dodge had an injunction served on his claim & quarts by the York Co who are claiming every new discovery found in the district. Smith & I had a time solving puzzels that we found in the paper.

April 5th Friday. I was a little surprised on going out before sun up and finding Tom Mathus employed by the York Co removing Dodges tools, windlass etc from his shaft and placing others there. I was to the Boon by noon, where I found Dodge with a small force urging the York Co to desist from this notorious intrusion which they soon came to the wise conclusion to do. All resumed its usual quietness. Evening I found *the Life of Lady Jane Gray* and was soon lost within its pages. All well.

Making Maps With John Gregory

Apr 7th Sunday. Clear and cold. I wrote a letter to Uncle Anthony Miller of Wyota wis. Started for the Boon stoped at Boices a short time and at Whipples the latter place I got my dinner. After which I made another start. Met Smith in Missouri City. Had an introduction to Mr. Gregory the discoverer of this Country. After reaching the cabin Dodge requested me to draw a map of all the lodes in sight as he wished it for evidence against the York Co. I drawed of the following Lodes with the assistance of Gregory, 'Vis', bob Tail, Nimeha, Log Cabin, Cotton, New Jersey, Fisk, boon, Black Hawk, Mammoth, Millwaukee, Vermont, washington and Monticello. Smith did not return. Thomas Mathws took tea with us.

Apr 8th Monday. Cloudy & chilly. Smith returned and we worked as usual. I went over and saw Frank Elder and went up to the P.O. Received two letters from home one containing very unexpected news 'Vis' Louis' marriage with Mr. Wm Campbell. I have only to say may their voyage through life be long pleasant and prosperous.

Apr 9th Tuesday. A stormy day nothing exciting. All worked. York Co. took possession of Dodges claim at 8:00 P.M.

Apr 10th Wednesday. Snowing quite hard. The York Co have a dozen men standing out watching Dodges claim. They all look sheepish and would be better off at home. Dodge came up and found how the ropes were working and had a few rough words with one of the Co in my cabin and were about to fight when I invited them out doors where they could have more room and there it ended and in less than an hour Dodge had fifty men on the hill who soon voted to have the thing settled by a regular process of law. We only worked half of the day.

Apr 11th Thursday. Clear & cold. All still this A.M. and we went to work again. Dodge compromised with the York Co. I wrote a letter home and drawed a map of several lodes which I also sent home.

The Hanging

Apr 12th Friday. Snowing hard but soon stoped & the wind took its place sweeping evry thing before it. We heard of a man being shot over in Lake Gulch last night and we all went over this A.M. to hear the prisnor and his victim & it was so cold that I concluded to go up to the office, from there to Whipples where I learned that John was sick and I went on up to see him... found him quite unwell but I think he will soon recover. After supplying his wants I returned to the Boon... the boys soon came when I learned that the prisoner had had his trial and was sentenced to be hung the 13th of this month. The prisoner seemed to care nothing about the deed that he commited thinking that he would be released on a plea of being drunk at the time. He has hopes of friends releasing him by mob. P.M. I sold Newland & brother 1 cord quarts for $40. We worked as usual. Quite cold & cloudy.

Apr 13th Saturday. Some excitment this A.M. The mountains & Gulches are lined with men going to see a man launched into another world for taking the life of a fellow man. The place selected for the execution was a small ravine putting out from Lake Gulch. There were some three or four thousand persons present and at a few minutes before twelve the prisoner was led upon the scaffold accompanied by the Sheriff, Judge, and two Ministers. The prisoner made a few brief remarks the ministers prayed and talked with him some time and then shaking hands with him left the scaffold. About the same time a voice was heard in the multitude in behalf of the prisoner he at first found sympathizers but after the Judge made a few remarks and put to vote what should be done it was soon decided that the prisoner should receive his just reward. Accordingly the rope was soon put around his neck, a cap over his face and he was led on the trap which was soon pulled from under him and he was no more. This is the first capital punishment I ever witnessed and I trust it will be the last. Weather very disagreeable all day.

Apr 14th Sunday. One of those cold stormy days. George and Smith left and I being alone did nothing but think of home which was soon broken off by Mathews coming in. Him and I went over to Frank Elders cabin and I gave him an introduction and a recomend to Frank which was the cause of his getting a good situation at work. George & Smith returned in the evening bringing *the Life of Lady Jane Gray.*

Apr 15th Monday. I made three trips to town and on to the blacksmith shop before noon. P.M. I borrowed $20 in dust from Frank and went up to the P.O. and got the boys some letters. I saw John at whipples where he is boarding at $6 per week. I had an introduction to Mrs Adams. Came back by Central City after my paper. I feel like keeping still after going so much over the Mountains. Read in the eve.

Apr 17th Wednesday. George not very well therefore I went into the shaft to blast which I did without getting blowed up which was doing well. John, J. J. Smith and Sinclare were here during the day. McQuitly a friend of smiths was here at noon. I went after a pail of water and lost the pail in a shaft 40 feet deep which caused me to climb down without any help but I made the riffle. Weather quite cold most of the day snowing in the eve. Read *Lady Jane Gray* and retired.

Apr 18th Thursday. George all right and worked as usual to day. I went over to Lake Gulch to get some retort but could not. From there I went over a high mountain which divides Lake from Gregory Gulch. I saw Newland who gave me but little satisfaction in regard to dust but made faithful promises which are numerous. In the evening we had a great time jumping in the cabin just for exercise but soon got sick of it

Lost in Shakespeare

Apr 19th Friday. The Boys went to work as usual, I went up to Missouri City P.O. from there down through Central City where business is quite lively. And some excitment about war between the North and South which is the topic of the day at present. I fear that nothing but fighting can settle the existing difficulties in the United States. Slavery seems to be the main cause of the South withdrawing from the Union. Weather warm and pleasant.

Apr 20th Saturday. We worked until noon when our powder gave out. P.M. we made preparations to timber up the shaft. Rained and thundered hard for the first time here. I went up with John to the old cabin. Rich brought our cattle off from the ranch. After taking a genral wash, retired, not very well contented.

Apr 21st Sunday. John and I went around the mountain to see the cattle found them in rather a poor conditon. Got back to the cabin after quite a walk and commenced reading but soon found ourselves lost in the land of nod which was disturbed by Robert Hammond knocking at the door.

Apr 22nd Monday. I started early this A.M after the cattle to draw timbers to crib up the shaft. John and Frank assisted with the work. Sold the cattle to Townsend for $75.00. Got back home very tired.

Apr 23rd Tuesday. We worked steady all day. Saw nothing exciting. I rented a cabin from Meuse near the Bob Tail Lode. A few are starting for the Blue River Mines 60 miles south. Got lost in *Shakespeare* most of the evening.

Apr 24th Wednesday. We finished cribing and cleaned out the shaft A.M. P.M. we moved over in the cabin that

I rented. Had several visitors during the evening. I went down to Gregory and borrowed $5.00 from Dodge on account of not getting any from Newland. Finished a letter I started and retired.

Apr 26th Friday. Snowing very hard this A.M. but soon cleared off quite cold. heard from John about quarts that we have been having crushed again. They got the large amount of $8.00 for one cord. Heard exciting news from the States about attacking troops, more states seceeding & etc. & etc. Several visitors during the evening.

Apr 27th Saturday. John bought a set of blacksmith tools today so that George can go to work. Dodge made us a proposal to take out some quarts which I think we will except. This is the last night that George stays with us for the present. Since I have been in the rocky Mountains I have truly learnt the "toil and trial are grim school masters but a flush of hope can make them beautiful even as a sunbeam the rude mountain frost."

Forty Feet Underground

Apr 28th Sunday. Snowing a very little but quite warm. George went up home. I went to see what we could take out quarts at on the Millwaukee for Dodge. Found it a hard show. Came home and was lost in *Shakespeere* in the evening.

Apr 29th Monday. Did nothing but travel over the mountains. Went down to Gregry twice and then up to the old cabin to see the Boys. Found George at work in the shop. Came back by the office and got three letters 2 from home and one from Uncle Lewis. Wrote a letter to Charlie and commenced one to Uncle Robert Hawley.

Apr 30th Tuesday. I hired out this A.M. hoping that I will find a better pay master than myself. Worked on the Bob Tail for the Ladode Mill Co Frank Elder being foreman. Some kind man left us a late paper in which we found the latest news. Retired early.

May 1st Wednesday. I am working 40 feet under ground where there is a splendid crevice of black and blue pyrites of iron from ten to thirty inches wide... and pays from three to seven hundred dollars per cord, of cours a dosen of us have livly times and the day is gone before we know it. I finished uncle Bobs letter and wrote a few lines to Mother.

May 2nd Thursday. Every thing as usual in the working line. A beautiful day what I saw of it. I got the latest news from the states. nothing but rumors of war but not any fighting as yet but expect there will be evry day. Calling for volunteers from all the northern states... If I was at home I presume that I would be among some of them but I can not think of going yet.

May 3rd Friday. A beautiful day too much to be confined in a shaft 40 feet deep most of the day digging for gold. N. Banes came in and we had a game of euchre for passing time it being in the mountains.

May 4th Saturday. Nothing exciting to day only we are visited with one of those cold, stormy and windy days which did not affect me much. Went down to Mountain City in the evening got a late paper which contented me during the evening.

May 5th Sunday. Snowed and blowed steady all day consequently I stayed in the cabin and wrote Uncle Lewis a letter and read *Shakespear.* Rough times.

May 6th Monday. I worked on the Bob Tail during the day and to make out a good days work I worked half of the night for Dodge and Smith worked the other half by so doing we make $4.00 each. Saw nothing but work and was willing to quit. Retired early.

Very, Very Sick

May 8th Wednesday. I put in a regular day & half again which goes rather rough. I let John have $5.00 to go to Trail Creek which is about ten miles South west from here. All well. Retired early.

May 9th Thursday. Weather changeable... I was taken sick in the A.M. but worked until noon when I went to bed where I stayed until Sunday the 12th not knowing what I was doing half of the time. Alone most of the time.

May 10th and 11th Friday and Saturday. Weather cold and chilly most of the time. I was not able to be up. The Dr pronounces my ailment chile fever and says it will not last long if I am careful of myself. A number the boys were here to see me.

May 12th Sunday. I feel much better to day and am able to sit up a little. The York Co are pitching into Dodge again about the claims. Both parties were here during the day to see what I knew about the matter and found out that I would not make a profitable witness for either. John came down to see me. Snowing hard P.M.

May 13th Monday. Snow three inches deep this A.M. I am able to be out. Went up and examined some shafts for Dodge as he is determined to have me for a witness. Smith went up to the office and got me a letter from home in which I learned of the great excitment prevailing there about war. Most of the boys including a brother have volunteered. May success crown their efforts.

May 15th Wednesday. Concluded to go to work for two reasons first I cant stand loafing in this country and second I expect the Sheriff after me as Dodge's law suit come off today and being a witness in this country is anything but pleasant. Therefore I worked steady all day. And learned at night that the suit had been adjurned until next week. Cloudy and warm most of the day.

May 16th Thursday. I am on the sick list again but made out to get up and get breakfast and then retired where I stayed all day thinking of nothing but Mother and Home.

May 18th Saturday. I feel any way but well therefore I concluded a change of climate would do me good. So I started for Russels Gulch which I reached after resting several times. Found George at work in the shop all right and I learned that they had deserted the old cabin and were living with Col Gratiot. Rained, snowed, blowed, and thundered.

May 19th Sunday. I feel much better this A.M. The Mountains are covered with a thick frost but the melting rays of Old Sol soon caused it all to disappear and the day was beautiful. Col Gratiot gave us a history of his journey across the plains and mountains to California in A.D. 1849 which was very interesting.

May 20th Monday. I am all right with the exception of being very week. Went down to Missouri City after a few things for Col. Weather warm and clear. I notice a few trying to make gardens on the mountains.

Dangerous Mine Shafts

May 23rd Thursday. Worked a short time in the mill and then left for a place where there is more excitment, as Russels Gulch has completly gave up, every body has gone prospecting. After reaching the bob Tail, I went down to the City and purchased a coat. I intend going to work soon.

May 24th Friday. I resumed my old place in the bob Tail this A.M. Did nothing but hold drill all day. After work I made and marked a number of stakes. Perfect summer weather. Clear and warm.

May 25th Saturday. I received several blows from the hammer to day instead of the drill. I feel more like myself tonight than I have for some time. I was sick for a long time. All well in the evening.

May 26th Sunday. Wind blows very hard and cold... stayed in the cabin A.M. P.M. I went up to Russels Gulch accompanied by Lewis... found the boys all well. To Meeting which is something new. On my return I noticed a few wagons that have arrived lately from the states. Propriters look rather blue.

May 27th Monday. All went to work as usual this A.M. nothing exciting happened until P.M. when one of the Boys jumped on the rope and went fortyfive feet without any help... as no one had hold of the windlass... he was not seriously hurt and thinks that he will need a little help the next time he goes down the shaft.

May 28th Tuesday. A beautiful A.M. We did not work on the account of the shaft not being safe. I went up to where Kendal is at work and he gave me two letters from home one of them contained the pictures of Albert and Theodore that I was quite ancious to receive as I now have all of the pictures of the family.

May 29th Wednesday. George and I went over to lake Gulch from there I went up as far as the lake. I got a quart of milk which is quite a treat in this country.

May 30 Thursday. All worked as they should. I worked as usual shooting out timbers and having a jovial time. Went up to Central City in the evening where business is livly. Left some gold to have Louisa a ring made. All well. Heard some singing.

May 31st Friday. I worked all day and half of the night therefore did not see much day light. Heard of no late war news. The last day of May was well put in made 3.75. So good by May.

Summer Brings Snow

June 1st Saturday. I put in a blast to day that knocked down most of the timbers in the digings. Smith brought certificates of 57 quarts claims for me to sell or act as agent for him as he intends starting south soon. Rained quite hard most of the day.

June 2nd Sunday. I went up to see the boys... found them both sick... stayed most of the day. Col made me a present of a fine pair of boots. Snowed very hard which will be surprising to the folks at home. Read in the evening.

June 3rd Monday. Cold & frosty. Worked as usual A.M. P.M. I went up to Russels district to vote and to see about having George to move his shop down on the Bob tail also our baggage from the old cabin. Frank and I went to Central City after Grub.

June 5th Wednesday. I found my regular employment agreeable to day. George went over in Lake Gulch and bought lumber to build a shop with. We went up to the City to see a show but were dissapointed. Read *Shakespeare* in the evening.

June 6th Thursday. George put the shop up today. I worked as usual shooting out timbers and having a jovial time. I went to the office in the evening and got letters. Weather fine.

June 7th Friday. George got the shop all fixed ready for work and I think we will make a little more than wages. I worked all day and all night. Very warm on top of the ground but cool fifty feet under. George got a little work to do and a promise for more Monday.

June 11th Tuesday. George got up at midnight to sharpen drills. John kept me awake most of the fournoon therefore I did not sleep but little. Everything received its required attention. After finishing my days work I helped George in the shop until he got done. Weather never was finer.

June 12th Wednesday. All passed regular. Except a sad accident that happened on the load near where I am at work "vis" a shaft fell in killing one man and badly brusing two others. John reports times are livly up to Trail Creek. I took a genral tramp first to Central City then to lake Gulch from there to Mo City & then home and went to work and quit at midnight.

June 13th Thursday. I worked all day and all night. Col Gratiot John and J. J. smith were here at noon. We also had three visitors at supper time.

June 14th Friday. Retired at 4 O'clock this A.M. and got up at noon. I am working all night and half of the day now. Went to work at midnight. Sometimes, it is not as jovial as I thought.

Music, Theater and Dancing Add Spice

June 17th Monday. A fine A.M. Every body at work and business lively. I went to work in the day time again got my finger smashed to day so that I am not able to hold drill or strike but can fill tubs. I had quite a tedious time trying to arrange Franks books got them so they can be understood and that is all.

June 19th Wednesday. All passed as usual A.M. P.M. I hired a man in my place while I went up to Virginia District to see a set of Black-Smith-Tools. Rained quite hard as I came back. I tried to find some iron large enough to make picks but could not. Read in the evening.

June 20th Thursday. Cloudy most all day. The night hands got scared out last night. The day hands are working as usual. Went to Central City and got a box of ointment for my finger which is painfull. Tried to read in the evening.

June 22nd Saturday. We received some exciting war news from Missouri and the border states today. It is the general opinion that Missouri will be the seat of some of the largest battles. Nothing but the old story to write about work & etc.

June 24th Monday. I am working sixty feet underground now where it is any-thing but safe. All passed smoothly in the shop and lode, George has to get up regular at midnight to sharpen tools. I went to the city in the evening to get some drugs to use in tempering tools. Heard some fine music from the Theater Band.

June 28th Friday. I think the rainy season has commenced. Rained quite hard to day our cabin leaks a little which is not pleasant. We went to the city in the eve.

June 29th Saturday. All worked as usual through the day. I went down to see Dodge in the evening... from him to Central City where I found some excitment about the theater. There paid a dollar and went in and was very well entertained until midnight. Retired.

July 2nd Sunday. I got up this A.M. feeling worse than when I retired for I sleeped in Smiths cabin on a bed that consisted of two blankets and pine Boards three inches apart. George not well. My finger is so that I can go to drilling again.

July 3rd Wednesday. A little of evry thing was going on to day in the lode in the way of fun and talking about what was to be done on the 4th etc. Rained.

July 4th Thursday. The old stars and stripes are floating in every direction this A.M. Most of us worked until P.M. when I went over to Lake Gulch and then to Central City where I joined the rest of the Boys and of course had a jolly time. Saw a few gents rather light headed. Went to the Theater in the eve where we enjoyed ourselves not very well. I think the next 4th I will try and attend a party.

July 5th Friday. Nothing but sleepy eyes to be seen this A.M. therefore not much excitment to day. I helped George in the shop. Times are livly and the Boys are getting all right again after the 4th.

Visiting the Young Widow

July 7th Sunday. A beautiful A.M. not a cloud to be seen. I wrote two letters and went to the office with them, and down through Central City and up on the side of a mountain where I found some fine strawberries. Several in the cabin.

July 8th Monday. I occupied a part of the day in fixing up the books for Frank and worked on the lode the remainder. George is doing well. Our wages amounted to $15.00 today. Went on the shift again therefore I worked all day and night.

July 9th Tuesday. I awoke at noon by Georges help. I fixed up the cabin and then made out half a dosen blacksmith bills and went to see what I can get on them which was nothing but promises. We have $175 at present. Went to work as usual.

July 12th Friday. I went up to the P.O. and received a letter from Charles which contained a flag sent by Mother. Went down to Central City after grub. John came down this evening.

July 13th Saturday. I got up early to help John make out blacksmith bills against men in the Russels Gulch. I went down to Central City to get a copper bottomed pan to prospect with. I worked until 12.

July 16th Tuesday. I went up to Russels Gulch to see if I could not get a little retort. I got enough to pay for going. Came back by Central City. Nothing going on there.

July 17th Wednesday. I was sick all day did not go any where or do anything. Went to work at night.

July 18th Thursday. Worked with George P.M. John came down. Had a little joke on me going to see the widow.

July 21st Sunday. Read the presidents message. Went up to Mrs. Crandalls (the Widow) a half dosen boys watching me. Had a sociable chat.

July 22nd Monday. I made out some blacksmith bills and went dunning with poor success as I only got $5.00 out of $75.00. I went down North Clear Creek three miles to see Dodge. George is talking of making a trade with Carr for a horse and $60.00 for the undivided half of what claims he owns here. I was up to Mrs. Crandals a short time. Worked all night which does not suit me.

July 23rd Tuesday. Is beautiful and warm George & I went down town and bought a bar of iron to make picks of. John sent me a copper bottomed pan to prospect with. Went to work again as usual.

Soldiers Readying for War

July 24th Wednesday. I helped George make picks P.M. Ed More took tea with us. I tryed prospecting but did not get a color. So I went to work.

July 25th Thursday. I got up at noon worked in the shop until time to go to work in the Lode. Had a noisy time in the way of singing at night. I fixed up the blacksmith book & time book at midnight. I keep the time of twenty six hands.

July 26th Friday. I did not go anywhere or see anyone worked half of the day & all night as usual.

July 27th Saturday. Had a hard old time this afternoon. I worked in the shop until 3 O'clock and then started for the four mile ranch after the horse that George has traded for. I lost my way and after travling over mountains sometime came out all right. After some trouble to catch the horse I started home. Arrived safe.

July 29th Monday. I had a fine ride this A.M. went up to Russels Gulch, then back and over to the ranch where I left the horse. Came back by Missouri Gulch. Went up to Central City to buy a wagon but did not. Went home & then after my washing.

July 30th Tuesday. Cloudy and rain quite hard most of the day. I went to work on the Lode again. The hands worked better than usual. I got up a subscription paper for Mrs. Brown who had her husband killed by the falling in of a shaft some time ago.

Aug 1st Thursday. I went down to see Dalton about a little retort but soon found that he had none. Went up to Central City where I saw a fine company of soldiers ready for war. Heard the fif & drum which almost tempted me to join but I concluded to wait a while and if I join at all I will go home. George is bound for home this fall. I should like to be with him but the retort is most too scarce yet.

Flooding Shafts

Aug 2rd Friday. I went to work in the Lode this A.M. Rained quite hard P.M. More & Townsend were here a short time. I got the subscription of Mrs. Brown in circulation and got $40 to start with.

Aug 3rd Saturday. I worked as usual. Rained during the day. I went down to Black Hawk Point with it but could not get any money. Went up to the City and then home & then after my washing.

Aug 4th Sunday. A very fine A.M. I wrote a letter to Miss Lucinda Millian. Went to the office and then down Clear Creek to Dodge's Mill after mony which I got. Got home and found Al Boiece there who stayed all night with us and helped us enjoy one of the hardest rains that I have seen for some time.

Aug 5th Monday. Everybody up bright & early to see what the heavy rain did... most evry one found their shafts drowned out. I diped water all day. Rained hard.

Aug 6th Tuesday. Cloudy and cold all day. Rained quite hard P.M. All worked as usual. I went down to the City and heard Hon H. P. Bennet make a speech as he is delegate to Congress and a strong union man. As his opponent went to answer him the building caved in giving some of them the head-ache but not seriously. They removed to the street where they had an exciting time for a few moments. George gets up regular every night to sharpen drills.

Aug 7th Wednesday. We had a fine rain this afternoon. I took Mrs. Brown the money that I got on the subscription $55.00 signed & $47.00 aid which she got. Worked as usual.

Aug 9th Friday. Nothing worthy of note. Today the work went as usual. Went down to the City saw some fun, Auction, Theater, etc.

Aug 10th Saturday. Cold and chilly. No rain but cloudy. I did not work in the lode but helped Frank settle up with a Dutch blacksmith. Made out the time of the hands and paid them some money for Frank.

Black Hawk Shows Up

Aug 11th Sunday. I feel anything but well this A.M. Went over to Whitmans cabin and around by the Lake to Central City and then home. Black Hawk with us at tea time. Weather cold & clear.

Aug 12th Monday. Finds us all well and ready for work. John came down and reports times dull. We kept George awake half of the night.

Aug 16th Friday. Rained a very little this A.M. The Boys got home early this A.M. some of them being on a general spree lost. Frank lost $154 or had it stolen he does not know which. Black Hawk started for the vally to buy us another horse taking the one we have with him. Went down to the Carrs cabin in the evening.

Aug 17th Saturday. Nothing exciting happened to day. No rain. Our rainy season is not near hard this year as last. I went up to Missouri City and around by Central where I found George and Mathews. Heard some fine music from the theater band and came home.

Aug 18th Sunday. George went up to Nevada Gulch to see about a wagon. I wrote a letter home A.M. and went down to Dodges Mill P.M. after money which I got. Sunday is all the day that money can be had. Went up to the Widows in the evening.

Aug 19th Monday. All found their regular exercise in the lode. And this being election day for Territorial Officers we all went down and voted in the evening. I saw no fights but heard of some very hard ones. Got home early. Read in the evening.

Aug 20th Tuesday. Nothing exciting only some of the boys got badly used last night and are not able to work this day. Several boys in the cabin during the evening telling stories and having a time in general.

Aug 23rd Friday. Only a few hands at work to day as the claim is not paying. Black Hawk got back to day bringing a pony with him for us which we paid $60. The cabin full during the evening. Black Hawk stayed with us.

Aug 24th Saturday. I hired Black Hawk to work in my place today. No rain. Our rainy season is not near hard this year as last. I went up to Missouri City and around by Central where I found George and Mathews. They & George went down town in the evening. I footed our books and found $268.52 due. Such is the life of a miner.

Leisure and Relaxation

Aug 25th Sunday. A beautiful A.M. The mountains covered with frost. John and I took a long stroll upon a mountain to see some of the lodes which looked very well after reaching them. Had a splendid view of the Plains & snowy range. As we came back I stoped at Capt. Bogg's mill and got a steam gauge. P.M. I started back home taking the same route I came and arrived in good time. Pony a little tired.

Aug 26th Monday. I went out to the Four Mile Ranch with the Pony this A.M. which gave me a fine ride also a fine walk coming back. Went to work P.M.

Aug 27th Tuesday. Cold & chilly all day. Rained P.M. and snowed on the range. I found the work all right. I went down to Central and up to Missouri City P.O. and got two papers from home. Col Gratiot in cabin all night. We had a long talk about the war news.

Aug 29th Thursday. Had any amount of fun in the Lode today. I went up to Missouri City and received a letter from Miss Lucinda Millian. Heard that the South had taken Washington but do not credit it.

Aug 30th Friday. Everything as usual on the Bob Tail Hill... some excitement about the war. I went down to the C.O.C. & P.P. Express Office and got a shot gun.

Aug 31st Saturday. The last day of the month, week, and Summer was a fine one. George has not much to do in the shop. We went to the Colorado Varieties in the evening. Not very interesting.

Sept 1st Sunday. Clear and cold the wind blows very hard. John and I went down to the city and had our pictures taken... went to a bakery and got our dinners and then George and I came home. I wrote a letter home and went to the office... back to Mrs. Crandles and then home.

Sept 3rd Tuesday. George is thinking about going home soon and he doesn't seem to care how things go. I went down town after grub and done some writing in the evening. Rained.

Ahhhhh... the Young Widow?

Sept 7th Saturday. All is well had an easy days work... rained P.M. Went up to Mrs. Crandles after my washing and stayed the evening.

Sept 8th Sunday. Wrote three or four letters in answer to some received lately. Went to the office and to town twice saw a number of men rather light-headed and heard of a law suit. Every body takes Sunday for trade, fun... with a few exceptions.

Sept 9th Monday. The usual routine was gone through with to day. Going to town, working & etc. & etc. Weather cold and stormy. Snowing on the range.

Sept 11th Wednesday. Nothing exciting only I had a general tramp calling on several... and got $3.20. Wrote and read all evening.

Sept 12th Thursday. A beautiful A.M. Work went as usual. I stayed on the hill in the evening but not at home was up to the widow's. Work went as usual.

Sept 13th Friday. Had a fine time during the day with the boys as they did not know where I was last night. I went up to the office and to Russels gulch to see Clark about some wood and to settle with Fasset. Got back somewhat tired.

Sept 14th Saturday. Cloudy all day. I stayed on the top all day as I had not much to do in the lode. Went up to Central City and paid a small debt that I owed for grub.

Sept 15th Sunday. Quite a heavy frost. George & I went up to Russels Gulch to see a wagon and got some specimens at the old cabin. Came back by Central City and got dinner. Went up to Crooks and had a fine feast of melons.

Sept 16th Monday. After the days work George and I went to the city to see about having some rings & pins made out of Rocky Mountain gold. After returning I went and settled my wash bill which was $3.00

Changes are Coming

Sept 17th Tuesday. George making preparations for going home. Bought a wagon paid $57.50. I did my regular work. John Cromby took dinner with us. I had a long talk with George about going home. Commenced a letter. Clear & warm all day.

Sept 19th Thursday. Had a fine snow storm to day but went as fast as it came. I went and got the jewelry this evening paid $6.00 for making... read an account of Jeff Davis's death... The President of the Southern Confederacy.

Sept 20th Friday. I worked A.M. and George took my place P.M. while I went and made a few calls on several debitors. Went down to Clear Creek & up to Central City where I saw several revolvers drawn but not used. Went over to lake Gulch... and never got a cent in all my travel.

Sept 21st Saturday. I was on the go all day went up to Missouri City and then up to the Patch claims after specimens and to see Kendal. From there to Nevada down Nevada to Central City where I got refreshments. Heard of a large battle fought in Eastern Virginia, a man being killed on the Burrows Lode and another commiting suicide in lake Gulch. Got back home and got supper wrote a letter home & retired.

Sept 22nd Sunday. Ought to be a day of rest but I find it anything else. I ran around to help George get ready for a start soon. Went out to the ranch after the ponies. John came down after the team to take Col Gratiot to Denver as he is very sick.

Sept 23rd Monday. I have been travling over the mountains all day trying to collect in what few debts that we have standing out as George thinks of starting home to-morrow. He went up to Russels Gulch to get the horses shod. He had a hard time. Tired after a long day.

Miners Returning to America

Sept 24th Tuesday. All excitment this A.M. as George intends to start for America. It took him and I all the fore-noon to collect on a few debts which were paid it being the last call. Soon after dinner we left the Bob Tail Hill my-self going as far as Denver with him... and five passengers to the river... the afternoon was quite stormy and disagreeable therefore the first half day was not very pleasant. Team worked fine and we reached the Guy House at dusk where we camped for the night.

Sept 25th Wednesday. Weather clear and fine. We got an early start and after climbing a mountain two miles or more commenced going down one five miles or more. Soon found ourselves at Golden Gate which is the end of the toll road. Passing by we soon came to Golden City where we saw a company of soldiers drilling which was all the excit-ment the place can afford. Here we bid the mountains adieu and find ourselves on the plains for the first time in a year & a half. Reached the Platte River at noon where we took dinner after which we went into the City of Denver which is much larger than I expected to find it. The Boys bought their outfit after some trouble and we came to the conclusion that Denver is not a very good place for trade and were it not for the soldiers that are now there it would be completely gone up. We stoped at the Elephant Corral. The boys settled up, and we all retired.

Sept 26th Thursday. I bid the boys good by this A.M. and they rolled out for America. George did not get to see John as he failed to get here according to agreeament. After taking a stroll around Denver I started back to the mountains. Got as far as the Green Mountain House and met John & Packard with the Col Gratiot so I turned around and went back with them to Denver. John and my-self went up Cherry Creek six miles to Allens and old acquaintances of ours and stayed all night had a socialble visit.

Sept 28th Saturday. We bid the plains farwell and passed through Golden Gate and were soon hid behind the mountains again which suits me much better than being on the plains. As our team was quite slow we did not get along very fast. John and Packard were bound to get to Smiths for dinner or kill the team which we came very near doing as they were about gone up when reaching there. We got a splendid dinner and were soon climbing the mountain again. Reached Gregry at sundown. Left the team at the Idaho mill and started for the bob Tail. Passed the evening writing and fixing the cabin.

Dull Times

Sept 30th Monday. John left for Trail Creek. I went to work on the Lode again this A.M. Locked up the shop as there is not work enough to hire a blacksmith. Went down to Central City and got some stationary, grub, & etc. & etc...

Oct 1st Tuesday. Snowed quite hard A.M. Blowed hard P.M. quite cold. I went down in the shaft to work. J. P. Bowling came to live with me to day. Wrote & read during the evening.

Oct 2nd Wednesday. John came down from Trail Creek to day on his way to Denver to see Capt Bogy who he has a note of $177.00 against. Bowling went with me to the City in the evening where business is lively. Cloudy.

Oct 4th Friday. Snowing very hard this A.M. and continued so to do all day and until after I retired. Sent up to the office and got two letters and & two papers all were interesting as one letter was from Louisa and the other from Miss Lucinda Millian. Read the war news.

Oct 5th Saturday. One of those disagreeable A.M.s. The wind blowing quite hard and snowed a little but we boys knew but little about it 70 feet under ground. Cabin full at night.

Oct 9th Wednesday. The ground covered with snow. I did not work to day but am going to work at night again. Went down town to see what was going on which is nothing of interest. Went to work at night. Still snowing.

Oct 10th Thursday. I retired a little past two got up at ten stayed in the cabin until working time and then went to work. Weather clear and cold.

Oct 12th Saturday. I wrote a letter home and went to work at 3 0'clock P. M. Quit at 10.

Oct 14th Monday. I commenced work this A.M. again. Some of the Boys were on a general spree last night from their looks I judge..

Oct 15th Tuesday. Every fellow at this post. I went down to the City in the evening... Auction... soldiers... and theater was all the excitment I saw. Came back and found a few Boys in the cabin... but did not stay long. Retired early.

Oct 18th Friday. Nothing worthy of note to put down for this days work. Weather never was finer & no war news.

Oct 22nd Tuesday. Nothing but the same thing to write over therefore I will not write.

Dancing is Tempting

Oct 23rd Wednesday. Fine working to day. Went down to Black Hawk Point in the evening. Read.

Oct 24th Thursday. Very windy... so much so that a black-smith shop was blown down...the boards carried some distance. All worked as usual. Wrote a short time and retired early.

Oct 25th Friday. Mr. Bowling got me up at five to breakfast which is rather early so I took another nap and he started for Denver. One of the Boys sick. I went up to Missouri P.O. got a paper. Came down by Central P.O. and got a letter from Bowling. Came home and read my paper through and wrote Miss Lucinda a letter.

Oct 26th Saturday. We did not get to work very early this A.M. and I climbed out of the shaft so as to quit at sun down. Black Hawk stayed with me all night. A nuget was found in Gregry Gulch worth 160.38 today. Wrote Uncle Robert a letter.

Oct 27th Sunday. Several in the cabin during the day. Mc-Ferrean and I went up to Missouri Flats to see some patch claim. I went to see Kendal came back by Central City and then home. Bowling returned... reports times dull in the vally.

Oct 28th Monday. Cold and very windy all day. The Mill Co were up to see the Lode... think the iron will pay well. I did some writing for Frank. Had a little excitment on the hill about a man stealing "retort"... came very near hanging him to a tree... but a friend of his beged for a new trial.

Oct 29th Tuesday. A beautiful day. All worked as usual. I went down town in the evening & went up to troters Hall where they were dancing... only stayed a short time for I could not stand the pressure of looking on.

Oct 30th Wednesday. A blast went off to day while we were in the hole injuring one man slightly only. Cloudy & snowed.

Oct 31st Thursday. Snow two inches deep & quite cold. I quit at five and went down to Black Hawk Point after Grub. Read a speech delivered in the Missouri convention by Hitchcock.

Nov 1st Friday. Some of the boys had exciting times about politics as one or two are a little tinctured with seceesh. Went over to Shaws in the Eve where I saw a young couple cradled and I judge enjoyed it tip top. Weather warm, clear and balmy.

Nov 2nd Saturday. Very windy and cold we did not get to work very early nor work very hard. A lady called on me to go and stay with her as her husband and number of others were come rather lightheaded and noisy. They soon arrived with 18 cans of oyster, peaches, sardines, and a pail of whisky, and had it not been for the lady taking sick they would of had a genral spree but they adjourned until to morrow. John was at the cabin when I returned.

Nevada City on Fire!

Nov 3rd Sunday. John & I wrote George a letter and I went up to the City with John who went on up to Trail Creek after seeing what was going on. Came back to Shaws where they were having a general time... I took dinner with the Boys and then Bowling & I went down to Pleasant Valley to Mr. Whitsides.

Nov 4th Monday. The wind never blew harder. About noon Nevada City was discovered to be on fire & before night was almost destroyed and the fire raging toward Central City which caused all the merchants to pack up their goods and teams were seen hurrying to & from dark until a late hour. I went down a few moments but the wind and smoke was so bad that I soon returned. Retired at midnight. Central City not on fire yet.

Nov 5th Tuesday. Many a poor fellow without a home this A.M. as the fire swept everything before it... Central City being saved only by the changing of the wind. Some of the Boys have new clothes this A.M. All worked as usual. Made out Franks account against the Mill Co. which is $2105.91.

Nov 6th Wednesday. The weather is fine as could be expected for the mountains. Nothing exciting.

Nov 8th Friday. Pleasant day all on hand and did their regular work. I was quite sick in the evening caused by chewing tobacco therefore I think of letting it alone in the future.

Nov 9th Saturday. Wind blowed very hard all day. Quite a fire on a high mountain but does not spread. The day passed as here-to-fore. Several in during the evening and Sinclare here all night.

Nov 10th Sunday. Cold and windy and snowed at times all day. Mr. Sinclare started for Boulder 18 miles north of here, and Bowling & I started for the Opal Lode five miles south east. Stoped at Whitsides in Pleasant Vally... had an introduction to Miss Agnes Randolph... and got Willis Reed to go with us as a guide. After climbing a very high ridge and going down one we reached the famous lode where we found Opals scarce however we succeeded in getting a few very nice ones and then started for home stoping at Whitsides for dinner. I went over to shaws in the evening and had a fine oyster supper, after which I went to Mountain City.

A Little of Everything

Nov 11th Monday. Calm after the wind of yesterday all worked except Bowling who is preparing for America. Frank came over and paid him $245 in dust. Sinclare here at night. Went to the city. Saw a little of evry thing and not much of any thing.

Nov 12th Tuesday. I talk of renting a claim on the Bob Tail. I made out the expense account for the Mill Co and worked in the lode the remainder of the day. Went up to Withrs in the evening to see Fretwell who is vry sick. From there to Nashes cabin where we tried to have a spiritual meeting but they would not favor us with a call. Weather clear & warm.

Nov 14th Thursday. Some excitment about going to America... none about war. Went down to the city after I quit work saw a little of evrything in the way of Theater, Auction, dancing, and occasionally a man slightly inebriated.

Nov 16th Saturday. Wind blowing a hurricane carrying snow & gravel with it. Stoped working the claim to day and am out of a job. Made out the hands account. Expect get a job soon.

Nov 17th Sunday. Went down to Central City got my dinner. Went up to Missouri mailed two papers and then went to see Kendal and then home. John came down. He is not doing or making anything. Weather clear and calm.

Nov 18th Monday. J. P. Bowling started for Illinois this A.M. I went to Lake Gulch with him. John went over to Chases Gulch and up to Trail Creek again. P.M. I repaired the cabin a little for winter. I with Elder and McFerrean rented a part of the Idaho Mill Co's claim on the Bob Tail for two months. I am living alone.

Nov 19th Tuesday. The wind blows very hard causing most evry thing to give before it. I worked a part of the day to get a good start Nels with me. Did some writing in the evening.

Nov 20th Wednesday. Weather fine. We hired two hands Gus Henry and Foster got along fine. We do our own sharpning which saves $10 per week. Went up town bought a keg of powder $12 and 100 sets fuses $2.50.

Nov 21st Thursday. I was glad to get down in the lode to work as the wind never blew harder or colder. Sharpened tools in the evening.

Nov 22rd Friday. There is a fine old war of winds on the range this A.M. but did not disturb us any. Worked as usual. I received a letter from Miss Millian and got my paper. Read in the evening.

Iron as Black as Coal

Nov 23rd Saturday. We took out half a cord of iron to day which is as black as coal. We have a crevise from ten to twenty inches of it. Samuel McClain stayed with me from Trail Creek. I wrote a letter.

Nov 25th Monday. Weather clear and not very cold we did not get to work very early but put in good time. The water troubles us a little. Read *Shakespeare* in the evening.

Nov 26th Tuesday. Snowing and blowing all day. We got in a good days work. Stayed home at night.

Nov 28th Thursday. As usual snowing and blowing only a little more so. Frank went down to the Mill and got some dust which I received two ounces of. Helped weigh out some for the rest of the Boys. Was over to Shaws in the eve. Read.

Nov 29th Friday. Stormy all day... so we were glad to stay under ground where we felt nothing of it. J. J. Smith and Sinclare with me at night. It costs me $6 per week including "cousins."

Nov 30th Saturday. Is very cold and windy... was glad to work for it is too disagreeable to do anything else. Stayed in the cabin contented with the eve.

Dec 1st Sunday. We had a fine rain storm to day, which is something the old mountaineers say they never knew before at this time of year. I wrote Louisa a letter went to see Root and Kendal... up to Central City where all is excitement about election. From there to Missouri City paid 25 cents for an apple. Mailed my letter and came home. Several in during the evening.

Dec 2nd Monday. It took some time to get the water out after which we put in a good days work. Election to day I did not go near as I had not time heard of several fights. Weather moderated but till windy.

Dec 3rd Tuesday. Experimented some on a pan of dirt from the Bob Tail without getting a color. We took out but little iron and a large lot of wall rock. Received a call from a Lady, which is a favor that all bachelors are not blessed with. Warm, clear, and fine.

Central City All Lit Up

Dec 5th Thursday. More snow to day, the weather very disagreeable so far. Every fellow hard at work. We sharpen the tools during evenings. I went down to the City in the evening.

Dec 6th Friday. Geo Packard here to day. Just arrived from over the range where he reports there is plenty of snow, game and some rich gulches. He got me a claim in one of them. I received a letter from Louisa. Smith here for a short time. Cold and windy.

Dec 8th Sunday. I did not leave the hill to day. Wrote a letter for Frank. P. C. Smith & several others were here during the day.

Dec 9th Monday. We got to work early & rolled out a fine lot of iron. Went down to the City & had a fine chat with Mr. John Campbell an old acquaintance of fathers. Central City well lighted up favors an eastern City a little.

Dec 10th Tuesday. Nothing but work. Stayed at home in the evening. Warm as could be expected.

Dec 11th Wednesday. Mr. Shaw made me an offer to go to the dance which I excepted. After work I went and for the first time in two years danced. The dance was similar to the state dances.

Dec 12th Thursday. The Mill commenced crushing our iron this week. Smith was here and I borrowed two ounces of dust from him. A. Anderson gave a me a call in the eve.

Dec 13th Friday. Wind blew very hard all day. Not much excitment on the hill at night as most evry one have gone over to Lake Gulch to a... DANCE. I did some writing & retired early.

Dec 14th Saturday. We concluded to take a rest therefore no work was done to day. The Boys all came up to the cabin where we had a general time and I judge from the noise that a few felt rather extra about... dark. Sinclare came down from Trail Creek. I did not ask him what he thought of the crowd for just about that time I did not care. Retired some time during the night.

Dec 15th Sunday. Got up with a slight head ache from some cause. Cabin looks rather rough but nothing more can be expected from a bachelor. Sinclare went to Missouri Gulch and back at night. I went up town saw a few sober men, got my hair cut. Came home read the *Presidents Message.* Cabin full of boys.

Bidding 1861 a Last Farewell...

Dec 18th Wednesday. Wind blew cold. Cloudy most of the day. J. T. Metcalf and Gus Henry who were working for us got blowed up but not seriously hurt. We sold one third of our interest to Foster for $120.00. Got the returns from our Iron paid only $152.00 per cord. Nels & I made $4 per day and foster came out about $40 behind. John came down to stop a short time. Frank & Shaw over. Retired some time A.M.

Dec 19th Thursday. Hired two new hands this A.M. in the place of those that got hurt. John concluded to go back to Trail Creek for a while. Nels & I were down town nothing exciting.

Dec 20th Friday. Snow steady all day. We got a keg of powder paid $12. Sold some gold dust at $16 per oz. I wrote Theodore a letter.

Dec 21th Saturday. Last night was the coldest that we had this winter. Cold & windy all day. Worked as usual all day. In the evening Nels & I went down to Mountain City. Called on Miss Hunters' and had a sociable chat.

Dec 24th Tuesday. Weather rough. All as usual until evening when three of us went down to the City to see Christmas come in which we did in style... that is easily remembered. Did not retire.

Dec 25th Wednesday. Retired at 4 o'clock this A.M. but did not stay in bed long. Went down to the City to see the fun vis. A Prize fight by men also by dogs all was fine ending in a free fight for all who wished to indulge. Most of them came away with a bloody nose sheriff included. I bought some clothes for New Years and came up to Shaws where we had a tip top oyster supper. I received a letter from Miss Millian. Retired quite early.

Dec 26th Thursday. Resumed our regular work this A.M. Were some time in getting the water out. Boys in cabin during the evening. Very cold.

Dec 27th Friday. I received a letter from home written by Father, Mother, and Louisa. Wrote a letter in the evening. Windy & cold.

Dec 28th Saturday. Nels selling out without consulting Foster or me but perhaps all for the best. Wrote some and retired early.

Dec 29th Sunday. I got part of my huge whiskers taken off for the first time since leaving home. Nothing exciting in Town. Weather warm and clear.

Dec 30th Monday. We were at work before light taking the water out got in a good days work. Wind blew hard all day but not cold. Went down to the City saw nothing very interesting.

Dec 31st Tuesday. The last of another year is about to depart with its varied scenes & changes. It finds me in about the same situation as last year... hard at work in a country that ought to be gold with out making but little. We put in a good days work. Got out some fine looking iron. Times are getting dull on account of powder being scarce. Weather clear & warm. I concluded to stay at home in the evening as I intend going to a party tomorrow evening. Wrote until quite late. Then biding 61 a last farewell I retired.

AND THEN...

Epilogue

After the last entry in his diary, Henry Hawley continued his mining operations for six more years, working in an extended area around Central City. Like many others, he finally gave it up, and went on to other endeavors. He kept books for several companies, and collected at least twenty patented mining claims, and many mines throughout the years.

In 1868, as a budding businessman, he went into debt $800 for a half-interest in a grocery store in the city. With his partner, Benjamin Lake, he had a flourishing business for a few years, after which the business changed to Hawley & Manville.

The notorious fire in 1874, that devastated most of Central City, destroyed their entire stock leaving them in debt $10,000. No ordinary man, Hawley remained undaunted, and the next morning after the fire, bought the stock of groceries from Roworth & Co. for $20,000, making their indebtedness $30,000 total. Over time he paid back every cent.

Buying out his partner in 1878, he incorporated the Hawley Merchandise Company. He erected the Hawley block, still seen today as the largest, most elegant building in the area. The business expanded to other locations, and was well-known for offering take-out orders and free delivery.

This graciously maturing Mr. Hawley became Gilpin County commissioner, member of the school board and stock-

holder of the Gilpin County Mining Association. He be-
longed to Central City Lodge No. 6, AF&AM., the Ancient
order of United Workmen, and the Gilpin County Pioneer
Society. At one time he was candidate for state senator
from Gilpin County.

He married Miss Annetta Miller, together raising a family
in their impressive home on Capitol Hill in Denver, Colorado. Ever true to his Central City, he ran his popular business there and was an important part of the community
the rest of his life.

When he died in 1923, at 84 years old, it was evident that
he was greatly missed. His obituary claimed, "He was well
known and esteemed by everyone, and his smiling countenance and hearty greeting will ever be remembered and
cherished in the coming years." Another stated: "Henry
was a patriotic citizen, a first class businessman, a man
of honor and integrity, one who easily made friends and
retained them for all time and one beloved by all who knew
him."

Upon his death, the diary was given by his daughter to the
Colorado Historical Society in Denver, Colorado.

Gracing the lawns at Fairmount Cemetery in Denver
stands the large granite Hawley tombstone. It is surround-
ed by markers of his family, and looks out at the panoramic
view of the Continental Divide and his beloved Rocky
Mountains.

*"I took a walk upon a high mountain where I saw a
grand sight below me. A very hard rainstorm while
the sun was shining bright and warm where I was."*

~ Henry Hawley

HENRY HAWLEY

From *Portrait and Biological Records of Denver and Vicinity, Colorado*
Chicago, IL 1898

GROWING UP WITH
GRANDFATHER HAWLEY

Annetta Ruth Lockhart, Henry's granddaughter, was interviewed in 1979 by his great-great-
granddaughter Linda Galbraith. The following is
a portion of the interview...

"My father's full name was Charles Edwin Wiley and mother's name was Mabel Clare Hawley (Henrys daughter). My paternal grandfather was Prentice Wiley and he was postmaster at Black Hawk. My paternal grandmother's name was Kate Tyler. My maternal grandparents' names were Henry James Hawley and Annetta Miller.

"We moved from Denver to Central City when I was young, and lived there most of my growing up years. My maternal grandparents [Henry and Annetta] had a very beautiful home on Capitol Hill in Denver and an apartment in Central City over the store. I loved to visit in Denver and loved their home there. There were the most beautiful, rich, dark red carpets, drapes and portieres, all to match, throughout the entire house. This home had five bedrooms and one bath. Isn't that something much different than today? However, they had toilets and a wash bowl out in what was called the 'buggy barn'... that's where my grandfather kept the surreys. The hired girl's room was at the head of the back stairs that led to the kitchen. My grandmother had a German girl who was such a wonderful cook and Grandma wouldn't let her girls (my mother and Aunt Dora) in the kitchen; they were 'ladies' and they should not be in the kitchen.

"After Dora and Mama [Henry's two daughters] graduated from high school in Denver, she sent them east to a finishing school and this is where they learned to play the piano and sing, and my mother could also play the violin. She could play most anything you would ask her, by ear. She really played the piano well and could almost make it talk. She could sing quite well, also.

My grandfather Hawley used to go to Denver almost every weekend and I very often went with him. The train left Central City on Friday at about five o'clock in the afternoon and I would go with him to go to the eye doctor the next day. On the way to Denver, it was a downgrade, and I never failed to get sick. It was a narrow gauge railroad and it had many turns. Anyway, we got there just about dinner time and we took the street car to their home. My grandmother had a very delicious dinner always. She was an excellent overseer for what she was going to serve and so forth.

"In fact, she was a perfectionist and had a good deal of class. For instance, we went shopping quite often on a Saturday when I was there. These trips lasted up into my teens and I'd come downstairs all ready to go and she would say, 'Ruth, put your foot up here.' (I wore high lace shoes.) Well, if one shoelace was twisted or if they weren't laced tight enough, she redid them. I thought I was being very careful, but, always, she had to redo my shoes. Anyway, she was always good, taking me to buy things and such. We always had to change street cars at what they called the viaduct. In this viaduct they had a little confectionery store and they served ice cream and sherbet and such. She would always buy pineapple sherbet (of which I am very fond). She also took me to the theater where they had shows and operas. This theater was in Elitch's Gar-

dens and did we ever have to dress for that! She had her
opera glasses with her every time we went to this theater.

"Anyway, that was the kind of life that I had with my
Grandmother Hawley and, in the summertime, I would
stay down there maybe two weeks and she would hire a
dressmaker to come in and make me some clothes while
I was there to be fitted. Every summer and every fall she
would have two or three dresses made for me and they
were all beautiful! I can still remember most of them. In
fact, I have a little kimono for one of my dolls that I made
out of the scraps that were left from one dress and it was
what they called challis. Challis was a very beautiful cloth.

"In Central City, when I was a young girl going to school,
my grandfather had the store in Central, as I have told
you before. Anytime I wanted, I could go in there and take
a bag and go upstairs and take all the candy I wanted. In
those days, candy was in wooden buckets and there were
many, many buckets upstairs in the store. Then, a few
times, some of us went to watch the ball games after school
and would stop in the store and get a big dill pickle each. I
was a spoiled brat there's no two ways about it!"

From family document held in archives at the
Gilpin County Museum, Central City, Colorado.

Henry   Annetta

SOURCES

Brief excerpts of the diary are found in the April, 1953, *Colorado Magazine*, published by the State Historical Society of Colorado. The article is entitled *H. J. Hawley's Diary, Russel Gulch in 1860*, pp 133-149, edited by Dr. Lynn Perrigo.

Photographs of Henry Hawley's original diary and first page of writing, from archives at the Colorado Historical Society Library, Denver, Colorado.

Gilpin County Map 1, *Guide to Colorado Ghost Towns and Mining Camps*, by Perry Eberhart, Swallow Press, 1959.

Photograph of Central City, 1859. Denver Public Library, Western History Department.

The biological excerpts entitled *AND THEN... (Epilogue)* are drawn from *Portrait and Biographical Records of Denver and Vicinity, Colorado*, Chicago, Illinois: pg. 459

Obituary quotes from *AND THEN... (Epilogue)* found at the Gilpin County Museum, Central City, Colorado.

Photograph of Henry Hawley, about 60. From *Portrait and Biographical Records of Denver and Vicinity, Colorado*, Chicago, Illinois: 1898, pg. 460.

GROWING UP WITH GRANDFATHER HAWLEY is a shortened version of an article entitled *GROWING UP IN CENTRAL CITY*, an interview of Henry's granddaughter by Linda Galbraith. It is found in archives at the Gilpin County Museum, Central City, Colorado.

Photographs of Henry Hawley and wife, Annetta, from archives at the Gilpin County Museum in Central City, Colorado.